Ancient Seals
and
the Bible

edited by

Leonard Gorelick
Elizabeth Williams-Forte

UNDENA PUBLICATIONS

A Publication of
IIMAS
The International Institute for Mesopotamian Area Studies

Ancient Seals and the Bible is volume 2/1 of **Occasional Papers on the Near East**,
a part of the system *Monographic Journals of the Near East*. Subscriptions available.

*This catalog was made possible in part by assistance from
the Archaeological Institute of America
and the Jewish Museum, New York*

ISBN: 0-89003-045-6
ISSN: 0732-6475
© 1983 by Undena Publications

UNDENA PUBLICATIONS
P. O. Box 97, Malibu, CA 90265

PREFACE

Leonard Gorelick and I first conceived of this symposium as a meeting of scholars to discuss ancient seals and specific aspects of culture and history within the lands of the Bible from an interdisciplinary viewpoint. It was to be connected with an exhibition on seals from Syria-Palestine to be held at the Jewish Museum in New York. The exhibition did not take place, but as the present volume happily attests, a symposium on "Ancient Seals and the Bible" was held at the Jewish Museum on December 17, 1982, and brought together five scholars. Their talks, in final written form here, reflect their varied fields of expertise in archaeology, art history, technology, history and philology.

In order to contribute to the advance of scholarship in a given field, symposia should occur at times of rapid reevaluation, disharmony and/or change.[1] Certainly such a reevaluation is occurring today in the study of the material culture of the lands of the Bible. An increasing literature advocates a Syro-Palestinian archaeology with methods, theoretical concerns, and goals distinct from those of Biblical archaeologists.[2] Important for this change in orientation is the discovery of sites such as Tell Mardikh, ancient Ebla, in Syria with its own writing and sophisticated culture as early as the mid third millennium B.C. These new archaeological discoveries have led to a reappraisal of past views of Syria-Palestine. No longer is it considered as a non-urban "country cousin"[3] and cultural province of Mesopotamia.

New methods of evaluating cultural change and new archaeological field techniques have provided alternate ways to evaluate the cultures revealed by excavation and the means to retrieve more complex information from ancient people's material remains. Critical for an understanding of the Syro-Palestinian region, for example, have been recent studies on the nature of nomadism, leading to a reconsideration of the frequent disruptions perceived in the archaeological record, formerly attributed to nomadic invaders.[4] Underlying the majority of these new precepts and methods is the concept that interdisciplinary collaboration is imperative for an understanding of ancient cultural processes.

As one of the most numerous artifacts available to us from excavations in Syria-Palestine, seals are uniquely suited to study by specialists in a variety of areas and valuable as a tool

[1] R. McC. Adams, "Preface" to *Seals and Sealings in the Ancient Near East*, eds. McG. Gibson and R. D. Biggs, *Bibliotheca Mesopotamica*, 6 Malibu, 1977, p. 1.

[2] For example, see: W. G. Dever, "The Impact of the New Archaeology on Syro-Palestinian Archaeology," *BASOR* 242 (1981), 15-30.

[3] J. A. Sauer, "Syro-Palestinian Archaeology, History and Biblical Studies," *BiAr* 45/4 (1982), 201-209.

[4] For example, J. T. Luke, "Pastoralism and Politics in the Mari Period: A Re-examination of the Character and Political Significance of the Major West Semitic Tribal Groups on the Middle Euphrates c. 1828-1758 B.C." Diss. University of Michigan, 1965; W. G. Dever, "New Vistas on the EB IV ("MBI") Horizon in Syria-Palestine," *BASOR* 237 (1980), 35-64.

for establishing the continuity or discontinuity of culture over time. They are engraved with scenes that yield information about ancient people, their environment, technological skill, and their socio-political and mythopoeic preoccupations. Inscriptions carved on the seals provide historical information, such as the names of specific rulers, cities or events, as well as data about the relationship of humankind to their gods and even one another. The material of which the seal is made, as well as the manner by which it is carved, are themselves "readable." Each can be used to reconstruct how—and how well—ancient man exploited local or imported resources to make his seals. The changing tools and stones used to form seals in turn reflect technological advances. Finally, seals and their impressions are employed as "index fossils," serving to date architectural structures, tombs or even archaeological levels in which they are found. Each of the five papers appearing in this volume is concerned with problems that address seals from one or more of these viewpoints.

The symposium "Ancient Seals and the Bible" was opened by my co-coordinator, Leonard Gorelick, who presented a comparison of textual references to seals in the Old and New Testaments, providing us with a broad overview of the uses of seals and their symbolic role in metaphor. In a similar vein, but from a slightly broader Near Eastern context, William Hallo surveyed both the lexical and literary evidence for seals from their earliest appearance through the first millennium B.C. In my study, I attempted to provide a new identification of the serpentine adversary and the weapon of the Syrian weather god.

After pointing out that neither the Bible nor other Ancient Near Eastern texts provide information concerning the actual making of seals, A. John Gwinnet presented the experiments conducted by him and his co-author, Leonard Gorelick, to determine the specifics of several problems in ancient seal carving, in particular the method of drilling these artifacts. Ruth Hestrin suggested significant new information on the officers of the court and royal functionaries who used the *lamelekh* seals. The final paper was given by Frank Moore Cross who discussed both the dating and provenance of one of the most important seals from first millennium B.C. Israel, the seal of Miqnêyaw, servant of Yahweh.

Initial enthusiasm and support for such an interdisciplinary symposium was provided by Joy Ungerleider-Mayerson, former director of the Jewish Museum. Much credit and thanks must be given to her and to her successor, Joan Rosenbaum, for bringing this project to a successful conclusion. The ceaseless efforts of Andrew Ackerman, director of the Education Department of the Jewish Museum, were instrumental at each stage of the planning and execution of the symposium and were critical in assuring its success. We are also grateful for the support and partial funding of this project and publication by a Regional Symposium Grant from the Archaeological Institute of America through the New York chapter of that organization. Finally, we would like to express our appreciation to the symposium participants and to Undena Publications for their help, efforts on our behalf, and expeditious publication of this volume.

ELIZABETH WILLIAMS-FORTE
University of California, Berkeley

TABLE OF CONTENTS

LIST OF ABBREVIATIONS

AfO	*Archiv für Orientforschung*
AHw	W. von Soden, *Akkadisches Handwörterbuch*. Wiesbaden, 1959-.
ANET	James B. Pritchard, ed., *Ancient Near Eastern Texts Relating to the Old Testament*. Princeton, 1969.
BASOR	*Bulletin of the American School of Oriental Research*
BiAr	*The Biblical Archaeologist*
BiOr	*Bibliotheca Orientalis*
CAD	*The Assyrian Dictionary of the Oriental Institute of the University of Chicago* Chicago, 1956-.
Diringer	David Diringer, *Le iscrizioni antico-ebraiche Palestinesi*. Florence, Monnier, 1934.
Herr	Larry G. Herr, *The Scripts of Ancient Northwest Semitic Seals*. HSM 18. Missoula, Montana, Scholars Press, 1978.
HUCA	*Hebrew Union College Annual*
IEJ	*Israel Exploration Journal*
IR	Ruth Hestrin, *et. al.*, *Inscriptions Reveal*. Jerusalem, Israel Museum, 1972.
IS	Ruth Hestrin and Michal Dayagi-Mendels, *Inscribed Seals*. Jerusalem, Israel Museum, 1979.
JAOS	*Journal of the American Oriental Society*
JBL	*Journal of Biblical Literature*
JCS	*Journal of Cuneiform Studies*
JNES	*Journal of Near Eastern Studies*
JRAS	*Journal of the Royal Asiatic Society*
KAI	H. Donner and W. Röllig, *Kanaanäische und Aramäische Inschriften*. Wiesbaden, Harrassowitz, 1962-64.
MIO	*Mitteilungen des Instituts für Orientforschung.*, Berlin.
MSL	*Materialien zum sumerischen Lexikon*
Moscati	S. Moscati, *L'epigrafia ebraica antica: 1935-1950*. Rome, Pontifical Biblical Institute, 1951.
Or	*Orientalia*
RA	*Revue d'assriologie et d'archéologie orientale*
RAI	*Rencontre Assyriologique Internationale*
UVB	*Vorläufiger Bericht über die Ausgrabungen im Uruk-Warka*
ZA	*Zeitschrift für Assyriologie*
ZAW	*Zeitschrift für alttestamentliche Wissenschaft*

INTRODUCTION*
ANCIENT SEALS AND THE BIBLE: AN OVERVIEW

LEONARD GORELICK

S.U.N.Y. at Stony Brook, New York

> Since the bible is a collection of writings, we shall naturally learn more about them from written sources than from unwritten. Yet, we must remember that writing without artifacts is like flesh without a skeleton and artifacts without writing are a skeleton without flesh.[1]

We share Albright's view in believing that artifacts, such as seals, can help bridge this gap between philology and archaeology. In addition, the pictorial representations on seals augment our understanding and involve us emotionally. Witness N. Avigad's response on finding seal impressions belonging to Baruch Ben-Neriah, scribe to the prophet Jeremiah and author of part of the Bible:

> I cannot refrain from expressing my own feelings when handling and deciphering these seal impressions for the first time. One has the feeling of personal contact with the persons who figure prominently in the dramatic events . . . preceding the downfall of Judah.[2]

To our knowledge, this symposium is the first on seals and the Bible. E. Williams-Forte, Andrew Ackerman and I believe that the subject has been neglected. One reason for the neglect is that it cuts across scholarly disciplines. For this reason, we have tried to emphasize the interdisciplinary character of the subject; papers are presented from different viewpoints, and include philology, art history, epigraphy and technology.

Another approach, one that will concern us here, is that of content analysis. In the Biblical Concordances, Tables 3 and 4 (see pp. 6-7) there are fifty-eight to sixty references to seals and sealing; thirty in the Old Testament and about thirty in the New Testament.[3] I

*I would like to acknowledge the valuable suggestions made by the following: Elizabeth Williams-Forte, co-coordinator of the symposium; Morton Smith, Professor of History, Columbia University; Lee Benson, Professor of History, The University of Pennsylvania; and Cecilia Grossman, former curator of Judaica at the Jewish Museum.

[1] W. F. Albright in *New Directions in Biblical Archaeology*, D. N. Freedman and J. Greenfield, eds., Garden City, NY, 118.

[2] N. Avigad in *BiAr*, 42/2 (1979), 846.

[3] R. Young, *Analytical Concordance to the Bible*, 20 ed. New York, 1936, 1662 and J. Ellison, *Nelson's Complete Concordance to the Revised Standard Bible*, Edinburgh, 1957, 602. Both concordances were used. Some discrepancies were found between them. these were reconciled by including all references to seals as a separate listing, even if there were two in the same verse, e.g., Kings 21.8 and Revelation 7.4. Surprisingly, both omitted the well-known reference in Genesis, Chap. 38.18, relating to Judah and Tamar.

have categorized these references in two ways: references which are metaphoric, e.g., "It (the earth) is changed as clay under the seal" (Job 38.14) (Masoretic text); and references which are functional.[4] By the latter, I mean references to seals in their many uses, similar to those that have been identified in the cultures of the Ancient Near East:

> So I took evidence of the purchase both that which was sealed according to the law and custom and that which was open (Jeremiah 32.10) . . . and put them in an earthen vessel that they may continue many days (Jeremiah 32.14).

Furthermore, I have classified the functional uses of seals in two ways: bureaucratic and non-bureaucratic. The former includes the designation and delegation of authority and the protection of government property. It also encompasses the sealings of a law, or official acts of witness, and signature to an official contract or to the sale and purchase of government property. Non-bureaucratic uses are personal and unrelated to the control of the political economy. While they may also involve witnessing contracts or property transactions, these are private. Included, too, in non-bureaucratic usage are seals employed as votive offerings, amulets or ornaments, as burial or heirloom items, or as gifts and pledges.

When I made a statistical comparison between references to seals in the two categories, metaphoric versus functional, in the Old Testament and in the New Testament, a difference became apparent. In the Old Testament, about two-thirds of the references are to seals in their traditional functions. One-third are metaphoric. In the New Testament, the proportion is almost reversed.

TABLE 1

Functional Versus Metaphoric Description of Seals

	TOTAL	FUNCTIONAL	METAPHORICAL
Old Testament	30	20 (66.6%)	10 (33.3%)
New Testament	31	13 (41.9%)	18 (58.1%)

Why the difference? I would offer the following hypothesis. It seems to me that, for the most part, seals in the Old Testament relate to a time when the Israelites were a nation and required all of the bureaucratic controls and trappings of nationhood, similar to those present in the older surrounding cultures. According to Nissen, "Aside from writing, sealing was the most important part of the controlling mechanisms of the economy."[5]

By contrast, seals in the New Testament reflect a period when the early Christians had little money, less power and were not organized as a nation. They had no need for seals to exert economic or political control. References in the New Testament to what might be

---

[4] While the determination of functional versus metaphoric (Table 1) and bureaucratic versus non-bureaucratic (Table 2) is subjective, the few ambiguous references do not alter the unusual degree of difference found. For a modicum of control, the judgments of several scholars were compared. The outcome remained essentially the same.

[5] H. Nissen in *Seals and Sealings in the Ancient Near East*, M. Gibson and R. D. Biggs, eds., Malibu, 1977, 15. While Nissen was referring to the Uruk period, it was also true, perhaps to a different extent, in other periods as well.

considered bureaucratic uses have to do with an imaginary,[6] not worldly, authority or bureaucracy:

> ... behold the lion of the tribe of Judah ... hath prevailed to open the book and to loose the seven seals thereof. (Rev. 5.5.)

> And ... I saw four angels standing on the four corners of the living God. (Rev. 7.2)[7]

Indeed, only one of the references in the New Testament deals with a clearly bureaucratic, authoritarian use in the sense of our definition: Pilate commands, "make the sepulchre sure, sealing the stone and setting a watch" (Matthew 27.66). The remainder of the references in the New Testament relate to a fanciful bureaucracy as compared with a factual bureaucracy described in the Old Testament.

A statistical comparison between the references to seals of a non-bureaucratic or personal nature is also revealing. In the Old Testament 50% of the references defined as functional are non-bureaucratic or personal. In the New Testament none are personal. This would seem a clear indication that the older, traditional, personal seal use as defined earlier and described in the Old Testament was not significant to this poor and powerless early Christian sect.

TABLE 2

Bureaucratic Versus Non-Bureaucratic Description of Seals

	TOTAL	BUREAUCRATIC	NON-BUREAUCRATIC
Old Testament	20	10 (50%)	10 (50%)
New Testament	13	13 (100%)	0 (0%)

With regard to metaphoric references, the differences between those found in the Old and New Testaments are not only quantitative, as shown in Table 1, but also qualitative: they differ in image or content. This is understandable, since it is conventional wisdom that metaphoric references stem from life experience, or "sitz-im-leben." Obviously the conscious events experienced by the authors of the Old Testament differed from those encountered by the authors of the New Testament. In the New Testament, for example, Babylon is a metaphor for Rome, and a door, an opening for missionary work.

One explanation given for the development of this type of ambiguity is that it stemmed from the persecution experienced by the early Christians. It caused them to develop protective methods which included symbols in art and a particular type of metaphor in language:

> ... out of ... extreme oppression appeared a fantastic type of literature ... which deeply colored the spiritual life of the Jews and early Christians. ... Since during periods of persecution clear speech often brought a death sentence, a secret set of symbols was developed ... and a language within a language.[8]

---

[6] Personal communication, Professor Morton Smith, Columbia University.

[7] M. Smith, *Jesus the Magician*, New York, 1978, 4.

[8] *The Dartmouth Bible*, R. B. Chamberlain and H. Feldman, eds., Boston, 1961, 712-713.

A totally different scholarly view, which readily acknowledges the special Christian form of expression, argues that it must have been comprehensible to all, or else Christianity would not have achieved its wide popular acceptance.[9] A further discussion of these metaphors is outside the scope of this paper. However, it is interesting to note that seals lend themselves to metaphor, not only in the Bible but also in the writings of subsequent periods and cultures. The most outstanding examples of this are in the works of Shakespeare. Of ninety-five references to seals in Shakespeare, approximately thirty are metaphors. One evocative example is from Sonnet 11:

> She carved thee for her seal
> and meant thereby
> Thou shouldst print more
> not let that copy die.

It seems to me that the metaphoric reference cited from Job "that the earth is changed as clay under the seal" was written by someone who either used seals himself or closely observed their use. It is interesting that the language of the Old Testament never qualifies the word for seal "HTM" in such a way as to clarify whether the reference is to a cylinder or stamp seal. A similar lack of distinction is true of the languages of the surrounding cultures, including Egyptian where the word for seal is also "HTM."

How do the functional uses of seals as described in the Bible compare with those identified in adjacent areas? The following uses are known in the Ancient Near East and are also described in the Bible.

1. To designate authority (Kings 21.08)
2. To seal letters (Kings 21.08)
3. To seal a covenant (Nehemiah 9.38)
4. To delegate authority (Esther 2.8)
5. To seal a law (Isaiah 8.16)
6. To seal a purchase or sale (Jeremiah 32.10)
7. To seal a door (Daniel 12.17)

The following are identified in the Bible but not in the Ancient Near East:

1. As a pledge (Genesis 38.18)
2. To seal a book (Daniel 12.4)

The following uses are known in the Ancient Near East, but are not described in the Bible.

1. As amulets
2. As heirlooms
3. As votive objects—in which the inscription can be read directly without imprinting.
4. As a gift
5. For deposition in a temple
6. For burial
7. To seal windows
8. To imprint the necks of vessels and on stoppers.

[9] W. M. Ramsay, *The Letters of the Seven Churches of Asia*, Michigan, 1963, 51.

In summary, then, whether functional or metaphoric, it is clear that seals were a most important part of the "Lands of the Bible" and of the Bible itself. They are echoed in our daily language, such as "a seal of approval," and in the common but perfunctory use, as in the notarization of documents, or in the Hebrew New Year's greeting on Rosh Hoshana—which expresses the hope that one will be listed and sealed in the Book of Life. Seals have been aptly titled by scholars as "The Mark of Ancient Man,"[10] and as "An Art in Miniature."[11] May they continue to roll and to impress us.

TABLE 3
Old Testament — King James Version

NO.	CHAPTER	VERSE	METAPHOR	FUNCTIONAL	BUREAUCRATIC	NON-BUREAUCRATIC
1.	1 Kings	21.8		1	1	
2.	1 Kings	21.8		1	1	
3.	Job	38.4	1			
4.	Job	41.15	1			
5.	Song of Solomon	8.6	1			
6.	Song of Solomon	8.6	1			
7.	Deuteronomy	32.34		1	1	
8.	Nehemiah	10.1		1	1	
9.	Nehemiah	9.38		1	1	
10.	Esther	8.12		1	1	
11.	Esther	8.8		1	1	
12.	Esther	8.10		1	1	
13.	Job	9.7	1			
14.	Job	14.17	1			
15.	Job	33.16	1			
16.	Job	37.7	1			
17.	Isaiah	8.16		1	1	
18.	Isaiah	29.11		1		1
19.	Isaiah	29.11		1		1
20.	Jeremiah	32.10		1		1
21.	Jeremiah	32.11		1		1
22.	Jeremiah	32.14		1		1
23.	Jeremiah	32.44		1		1
24.	Ezekiel	28.12	1			
25.	Daniel	9.24	1			
26.	Daniel	12.4		1		1
27.	Daniel	12.9		1		1
28.	Daniel	6.17		1	1	
29.	Daniel	6.17		1	1	
30.	Genesis	38.18		1		1
	TOTAL:	30	10	20	10	10

[10] M. Noveck, *Ancient Near Eastern Stamp and Cylinder Seals: The Gorelick Collection*, exh. cat. Brooklyn Museum, Brooklyn, New York, 1975, 1.

[11] E. Porada in *Sumerian Art in Miniature, the Legacy of Sumer*, D. Schmandt-Besserat, ed., Malibu, 1976, 107 ff.

TABLE 4
New Testament — King James Version

NO.	CHAPTER	VERSE	METAPHOR	FUNCTIONAL	BUREAUCRATIC	NON-BUREAUCRATIC
1.	Romans	4.11	1			
2.	Romans	15.28	1			
3.	Timothy	2.19	1			
4.	Revelations	5.1		1	1	
5.	Revelations	5.1		1	1	
6.	Revelations	5.2		1	1	
7.	Revelations	5.5		1	1	
8.	Revelations	6.1		1	1	
9.	Revelations	6.3		1	1	
10.	Revelations	6.5		1	1	
11.	Revelations	6.7		1	1	
12.	Revelations	6.9		1	1	
13.	Revelations	6.12		1	1	
14.	Revelations	7.2	1			
15.	Revelations	7.3	1			
16.	Revelations	7.4	1			
17.	Revelations	7.4	1			
18.	Revelations	7.5	1			
19.	Revelations	7.6	1			
20.	Revelations	7.7	1			
21.	Revelations	7.8	1			
22.	Revelations	8.1		1	1	
23.	Revelations	9.4	1			
24.	Matthew	27.66		1	1	
25.	John	3.33	1			
26.	John	6.27	1			
27.	2 Corinthians	1.22	1			
28.	Ephesians	1.13	1			
29.	Ephesians	4.30	1			
30.	Revelations	20.3	1			
31.	Revelations	22.10		1	1	
	TOTAL:	31	18	13	13	0

"AS THE SEAL UPON THINE ARM":
GLYPTIC METAPHORS IN THE BIBLICAL WORLD

WILLIAM W. HALLO

Yale University

In one of the more enigmatic chapters of Genesis, Judah paid Tamar for certain services she rendered him with a most intriguing I.O.U.: his seal, his cord, and the staff in his hand. A little later in the narrative, these items served to identify him (Gen. 38:18,25).

In the story of Joseph which surrounds this strange episode, a seal by another name again plays an interesting role, this time as the sign of royal authority conferred on Joseph by Pharaoh (Gen. 41:42).

Both the Hebrew words for seal *hôtam* (resp. *hôtemet*) in the story of Judah, *ṭabba'at* in the romance of Joseph, are well known through most of the Biblical world. Both have been traced to Egyptian origins by Lambdin (1953) or to the stock of age-old cultural terms (*Wanderwörter*) which travelled across the Ancient Near East with the objects they designated by Rössler (1952.132f.).

And indeed seals are an early hallmark of Near Eastern civilization, first in stamp form and, before the end of the fourth millennium, in cylinder form. But they are most characteristic of Mesopotamia, and I hope to be able to use some of the lexical and literary evidence of that ancient land and its environs in order to throw additional light on the various roles played by seals in Biblical narratives and imagery, thus taking matters beyond the point where they were left by Moscati in the first survey of the subject (1949).

In Mesopotamia, the earliest attested word for seal is the Sumerian kišib. Its phonetic shape suggests that it belongs to the substrate vocabulary of the early chalcolithic age according to Salonen (1968:5,11; 1969:110), i.e., as early perhaps as the sixth millennium B.C. (Salonen 1972:8f.). That happens to be also the date of the earliest published stamp seals from Mesopotamia, though their floruit was only reached in the second half of the fourth millennium (Buchanan 1967:265-7 by comparison with Porada 1965:175f.). By the end of the fourth millennium, the pictographic forerunner of the cuneiform sign for seal can be identified among the archaic texts from Uruk and Jemdet Nasr; it is said to represent a combination of a writing-reed and a clay-tablet ruled into cases (Deimel 1928-33:138:1 and 314:4; but cf. Falkenstein 1936 Nos. 553, 639f.).

The equivalent Akkadian term for seal or sealed tablet (*kunukku*) is said to be attested as early as the middle of the third millennium if we may believe the evidence of a lexical text from Ebla which equates "Sumerian" NÍG - ki-nu-ki with "Eblaite" *hu-tà-mu* (Pettinato 1982 p. 37 iii 13f. = p. 201:40b), i.e., presumably "sealed object," but this evidence for a possible loanword is at best extremely ambiguous.[1]

---

[1] Only one text has this equation; the others have instead níg-šè- nu-šè = *su-mu-tum*.

Egyptian, in addition to the common terms for (stamp) seal (*ḏb 'tt*) and seal (ring) (*ḥtm*) already alluded to, has a rarer term specifically for the cylinder seal (*śḏ3.t*) (Schott 1957). This may just possibly be the source of the Hittite word for seal (*šiịatar*) but more likely that represents an abstract noun derived from the verb *šiịa* — "to show (identify?) oneself" (Friedrich 1952 s.v.).

But let us leave these lexical details and consider what the larger literary context can tell us about the various roles which seals played in real life and therefore the kinds of significance which their metaphoric usage took on in the Biblical world.

In one sense the most basic, perhaps, indeed, the original significance of the seal, was legal: it emerged, together with the emergence of capital formation, as a mark of ownership or contractual obligation by an individual, in effect as a symbolic representation of the individual. Small in size and easily carried on the person, it was readily available to be impressed or rolled on the wet clay of a vessel or tablet. The case of Judah with which we began is a reflex of this legal concept: in leaving his seal, Judah left a part of himself which established both his identity and his legal obligation to redeem the pledge he had made.

Mesopotamian legal and omen literature amply documents this aspect of the seal, most intriguingly in the negative case of the loss of a seal (Hallo 1977 and 1981; Muhly 1981). Whenever that unfortunate event occurred, the contract provided that any tablet that in future might turn up with an impression of the lost seal was to be considered null and void; it was in fact (in modern parlance) to be shredded. If the hapless seal owner was sufficiently prominent, his loss was even the subject of a public pronouncement by the official herald throughout the city streets.[2]

In the vast omen literature of Mesopotamia, the loss of a seal involved (like most other contingencies) a generally unfavorable prognosis. In particular the dream omens tended to equate the loss of a seal with the death of a son or daughter. And there were suitable rituals to ward off the evil portended (Hallo 1977). On one view, all this evidence points to "ancient man's intense psycho-social identification with his seal" (Root 1982:60).

Other provisions made by and for those without seals are equally instructive (Renger 1977:77). They might commission a seal cutter to prepare a cheap seal from clay, good only for the immediate purpose at hand. Or they might borrow the seal of a relative or friend—in which case that fact was duly noted (Schneider 1947). Most characteristically, they might substitute for the missing seal some other symbol of their persona, notably their finger nail or the fringes of their garment (Stephens 1931; Boyer 1939; Milgrom 1981). Like the modern finger-print, these substitutes were apparently considered equally valid with the seals as proof of identity.[3] By a curious process, the nail marks may even have become seals again if one can thus interpret the stamps with which to produce such marks and the corresponding impressions found at Kalah (Mallowan 1950:173; cf. Pohl 1951:254; 1954:181).

The reason for the unavailability of seals was, of course, not their occasional loss but their inherent value. Though small, they were delicately carved with a pictorial design and sometimes with an inscription, on hard and often semi-precious stone which, in Mesopotamia at least, had typically to be imported from abroad. Seals, therefore, were beyond the means of the common man and, at their best, were considered worthy of donation to the

---

[2] Note these additional examples and parallels: Owen 1975 No. 257; Roth 1979:54; Skaist 1980 esp. pp. xlix-li; CADṢ 186f.

[3] Owen 1975 no. 245 seems to take the practice back to neo-Sumerian times, but Römer 1978:190 *ad loc* questions this.

deity. This leads us to the second role of the seal: as *objet d'art* and, more particularly, as votive object.

Votive seals are well attested for all periods and over all areas of the Ancient Near East (Gelb 1977:120f. [XX]).[4] An example from the Middle Euphrates region even found its way to Beersheba (Raincy 1973). But they are particularly distinctive in ancient Sumer, where they are set apart from their more "practical" counterparts not only by their considerably greater size, costlier material and more elaborate decoration, but also by a special genre of votive inscription found only on the original seal, never on seal impressions (Hallo 1962:13f. and n.107; 1981:x and n.3) except perhaps in the case of those so-called divine seals (Opificius 1971 [a]) which served as "temple-seals" (Gelb 1977:112 and 125 [XXX]). Often enough such votive seals are inscribed in the positive sense, and were clearly not intended for impressing in clay. Their inscriptions, exactly like those of the larger votive objects, prayed for the life of the donor and/or his designated beneficiaries, and were no doubt deposited, like them, in the sanctuary in order to convey that prayer to the deity in place of the donor himself or his statue. Specifically, such seals will have been carved for the cult statue of the deity and are well represented in the inventories of the divine garments and accoutrements (Leemans 1952; Owen 1975 No. 152).

An equivalent role is played by seals in the furbishing of the Tabernacle in the wilderness (Exodus 35:22), for the rings brought by "men and women, all whose hearts moved them, all who would make a wave offering of gold to the Lord" are none other than the signet rings (*tabba'at*) which we already met in the Joseph story. They are here bracketed with broaches, earrings and pendants—much as in the expiatory offering of a portion of the booty to the Lord later in the desert wanderings (Numbers 31:50). That earrings were particularly prized as votive offerings and virtual idols in their own right is clear from other Biblical passages. At Shechem, they are buried together with the alien gods by Jacob before he returns to the land of Canaan from his sojourn in Haran (Gen. 35:4) and "are somehow the counterpart of idols whose influence must be disposed of" (Kingsbury 1967:136). They are used by Gideon to make an *ephod* which becomes a snare to him and his house (Judges 8:24-27). And in the form of nose rings they are again associated with signet rings in the catalogue of feminine finery condemned by Isaiah (3:21). No wonder, then, that excavations have turned up votive earrings as well as votive seals (Hallo 1983 nn.131-133).

But if the ordinary mortal could offer a seal to the deity, it was equally true in the Biblical world that, as a mark of special favor, he might receive one from his superior. The king himself bestows the seal on his chosen retainers in a distinctive design and inscriptional type known from Mesopotamia (Sollberger 1965) and Elam (Lambert 1971) at the end of the third and the beginning of the second millennia and variously designated as "presentation seals" (Franke 1977) and "office seals" (Gelb 1977 [XXI]). We are once more reminded of the investiture of Joseph and the parallel account in Esther regarding first Haman (3:10) and then Mordecai (8:2), each time signifying the delegation of royal authority to the vizier.

From here it is only a short step, via metaphoric expansion, to the concept of the seal as a symbol of personal reliance on and affection for the recipient. In the Bible, where God so often plays the role reserved for kings elsewhere in the Near East, this metaphor moves

---

[4] Two particularly interesting examples are Porada 1951 ("Abisare 2") and Oberhuber 1972:128 fig. 102 (Old Akkadian ?), both (?) dedicated by seal-cutters (bur-gul), as if to illustrate the description of the votive object as "an artistic replica of an object used in daily life" by the donor (Hallo 1962:12).

easily from the royal to the divine realm. In Jeremiah, God says of the hapless penultimate king of Judah (22:24): "If you, O Coniah, son of Jehoiakim, king of Judah, were a signet (*ḥôtām*) on my right hand, I would tear you off even from there."[5] In rather more positive terms, the post-exilic prophet Haggai concludes his message thus (2:23): "I will take you, O my servant Zerubbabel son of Shealtiel—declares the Lord—and make you as a signet (*weśamtîḵa kaḥôtam*); for I have chosen you—declares the Lord of Hosts." Both prophets imply the intimacy of the signet-ring with its finger and both presumably have in mind a stamp-seal set in such a ring.

This brings us to one of the most celebrated of all Biblical similes. In Song of Songs 8:6a we read: "Let me be a seal upon your heart, like the seal upon your hand. For love is fierce as death, passion is mighty as Sheol." Or, mindful of the wording in Haggai, we might also render: "Make me as the seal (*śimēnî kaḥôtam*) upon thy heart, as the seal upon thine arm, for love is strong as death, passion hard as hell." Franz Rosenzweig (1972:156-204) and Marvin Pope (1977:210-229), to name only two commentators, consider this half verse the very key to the message of the entire Canticle. But what is the sense of the simile? Must we eliminate the "seal upon the heart" as a meaningless doublet, or understand the "seal upon the arm" as a signet-ring on the hand? Some commentators would favor this course. But the comparative data can salvage the text as it stands.

The signet-ring (Akkadian *unqu* Sumerian šu-gur) was not known in Mesopotamia till relatively late. In its earliest form, therefore, the stamp-seal was worn, not on the finger like the signet, but suspended from a dagger, as in "the death of Ur-Nammu" (Kramer 1967 line 119) or, more particularly, from the wrist. Indeed, the very word for wrist in Sumerian (kišib-lá) means literally "seal-carrier," "(place where) the seal is hung" according to Cooper (1978:129f.; but cf. Hallo 1981:255f.) and its Akkadian equivalent (*rittu*) has been identified by Leemans as meaning "stamp-seal" when preceded by the determinative for "stone" (1952:10 and 1960:7; but cf. *AHW* s.v.; Hallo 1962:14 and n.112). Some seals excavated in Israel seem similarly to have been originally hung from bracelets (Hestrin, orally). [See also Pl. XII-1.]

But between the early stamp seals and the late signets, the typical form of Mesopotamian seal was not a stamp-seal at all, but a cylinder seal. And such a cylinder-seal was mostly not worn on hand or arm. Rather, it was invariably drilled through its long axis with a continuous hole designated to accommodate a pin which served two practical purposes. With the help of the pin the seal could, in the first place, be rolled in clay (much in the manner of a rolling pin used on dough), and, in the second, worn on the person. Initially, the latter purpose was apparently attained in combination with the contemporary mode of dress or, as Humphries has put it for the Early Dynastic III Period (ca. 2500-2300 B.C.): "at least at Ur the usual manner of wearing or carrying a cylinder seal was suspended from a shoulder pin which fastened one's robes together" (*apud* Rathje 1977:26 and n.8). But with the emergence of the fibula, or safety pin, in the second millennium (Hallo 1967:66:18 and n.5), the latter became specialized for its clothing function and it was found more practical to provide the seal-pin with an eye of its own and thus make it suitable for attachment to a necklace by which it could then be worn around the neck. [But see Pls. XII-2, XII-3.]

Cuneiform sources furnish a possible term for this pin. The oldest sign for "carpenter"

---

[5] Translations here and elsewhere after NJV (The New Jewish Version) (Jewish Publication Society 1962-1982) except as otherwise indicated.

(nagar) is a pictogram representing a chisel (Deimel 1928-33:560:1); with the addition of one further stroke (cf. Krecher 1966 n.409), the sign (now read bulug) comes to mean either "chisel" (Akkadian *maqqaru*) or "needle, pin, stake" (Akkadian *pulukku* or "sliver" (Akkadian *hiṣbu^B*) and, by extension, "border-marker, border" (Akkadian *pulukku, kudurru*). The meaning "chisel" is probably intended in the myth of "Enki and the World Order" (Benito 1969 line 406) and a number of other literary allusions (Landsberger 1967:207-209);[6] the meaning "border" is likely in the geographical name Pulukkû (BU= LUG.KI; cf. Hallo 1964 Par. 24) and elsewhere. But when such an object is associated with a seal, we are entitled to regard it as the pin on which the seal is mounted.

This is notably the case when particularly precious seals are involved, as gifts or otherwise. This occurs in the first place in a lament for the divine Dumuzi in which his sister Geshtin-anna offers to ransom him with her most precious ornaments, beginning with her silver pin and lapus lazuli seal (Jacobsen 1980:22).[7] It occurs in the second place in a "Love-song to a king" which counts among the presents bestowed by Shu-Sin of Ur upon his priestess-concubine, "a pin of gold and a seal of lapis lazuli" (Kramer in *ANET* 496 line 11).[8] It is met with further in archival texts from Ur dated to his son and successor Ibbi-Sin, the fifth and last king of Ur's Third Dynasty, specifically to the tenth month of his fifteenth year, when Ahu-waqar received from Ir-Nanna various amounts of gold on at least four separate days in order to decorate five seals of lapis lazuli, of which four were to be inscribed, including two which were "on a pin" (bulug-e; *UET* 3:617, 620, 623, 666). While lapis lazuli tablets are well known among the Sumerian deities (Hallo 1970 *ad* lines 1 and 30f.), the notion that these were such tablets somehow incised with a metal stylus (Krecher 1966 n.410) seems rather unlikely,[9] given the fact that numerous texts from the same year record transactions between the same principals involving other jewelry items including rings, lunar crescents, earrings, etc. (Loding 1974 *passim* and 1976 *passim*), and that the concept of inscribing a seal became so familiar that the very term for "inscribing" used here in Sumerian (mu-sar) was equated with "inscribed seal" (*kunuk šumi*) in Akkadian (Civil 1971:202:54; cf. Hallo 1977 n.23).

The pin so identified was particularly often given to women (Falkenstein 1964:91); it is thus conceivable that it formed a characteristic portion of the marriage gift, and even that it gave its name to the dowry in general, for the dialectical form of the Sumerian word (mu-lu-ug or mul-ug; cf. Krecher 1966 n.412; Joannès 1980:184 and n.6) may be the long-sought source of Akkadian *mulūgu* (Jacobsen 1980:24 *ad* line 6) which passed into Talmudic Aramaic in the meaning of "dowry" or "wife's estate" (*m^e lôg*; cf. Levine 1968, esp. n.5)—provided, that is, that loanwords from dialectical Sumerian into Akkadian are admitted as a possibility.

Of course not every last Mesopotamian cylinder-seal was necessarily mounted on a pin. Occasionally the older form with attached loop or "handle" on top (cf. e.g., Buchanan 1981 nos. 133f.) may have survived, to judge by an allusion to a "seal (with a) hand(le)" (kišib-šu) as a gift to an underworld goddess in "the death of Ur-Nammu" (Kramer

---

[6] Cf. also umbin = *imṭû* = chisel.

[7] Jacobsen translates "animal-man trinket" (mu-lu-ug) but the duplicate text noted by Krecher (1966 n.412) favors the rendering "pin" (bulug). See also below.

[8] Kramer translates "pendant(?)" but here Jacobsen (1953:47) prefers "pin."

[9] The confusion is due to the fact that the signs for "tablet" (dub) and "seal" or "sealed tablet" (kišib) are indistinguishable in the early orthography.

1967:119 line 109). And at other times, the seal was mounted, not on a pin, but between two "caps" (cf. e.g. Buchanan 1981 no. 1030; from the Kingdom of Hana on the middle Euphrates); such caps were apparently known as "headdress, helmet" (sagšu = Akkadian kubšu) and could be made of gold or semiprecious stone (Bottéro 1949:148:104, 170:354, 138:13; from Qatna in Syria).

But even such handled or capped seals could be mounted on a pin, as in the case of the lapis lazuli seal with gold cap presented by Kirikiri, king of Eshnunna, to his son Bilalama (Franke 1977:63f. and nn.21f.)[10] and, whether so mounted or not, could easily be attached to a necklace. This is clear from the votive seal which Marduk-zakir-shumi I, a ninth-century king of Babylon, presented to Marduk, and which is described in its inscription as "a cylinder seal of lustrous lapis-lazuli, which is firmly set in reddish gold, worthy of his holy neck" (Rainey 1973:65; cf. Goff 195f:31; 1963:204). In other words, "the seal proper (was) made of lapis lazuli . . . , originally provided with golden handles, . . . designed to be worn around the statue's neck . . . , (and) probably to be attached by means of a cord" (Brinkman 1968 n.1255).

Cuneiform literature provides many other references to votive seals worn around the neck (kišādu) of cult-statues of such deities as Uṣur-amassu (CADK 449 ab)[11] and Sin (CAD I-J 328b), as well as of kings (Rost 1893 p. 14:69), especially when accompanying a deity (Falkenstein 1959:40 rev. 12; cf. Oppenheim 1974:3498). But the custom is equally well documented for ordinary seals worn by ordinary mortals (CADK 447-449; 544). Of the many allusions in question, only one will be cited here, for it shows the very same metaphoric extension of meaning as the Hebrew expression. In a letter to the Assyrian king (?), we read (CADK 544c) "you placed him like a seal around your neck" meaning, apparently, you were on terms of particular intimacy with him.

Just so, in the Song of Songs, the beloved wishes to be as intimate with her lover as the two seals worn by him, the stamp seal carried on his wrist and the cylinder seal worn around his neck which rests on his heart. Only one each was likely to be worn by any one person; hence both times the definite article is called for and in fact employed.[12] We can thus understand the first half of the Biblical simile in light of the comparative evidence. But what is its connection with the second half? How does the image of the seal bridge the gap between love and death?

Here one may appeal to a further and largely neglected function of Mesopotamian glyptic, namely as funerary offering.[13] Together with tools and weapons, seals form part of the private possessions buried with their owners or contributed to their graves in many periods and regions of the Ancient Near East, though not as universally as ceramics and jewelry (Strommenger 1971). A detailed typology of the seals in the Early Dynastic III graves at Ur has, moreover, led to the tentative conclusion that they correlate significantly with the status of their owners; seals of lapis lazuli decorated with banquet scenes, for instance, seem to identify higher ranking temple or court functionaries than seals of shell decorated with

---

[10] Franke's assertion that this "is one of the few extant seals represented by ancient impressions" cannot be tested against my rule (apud Buchanan 1981 p. xii and nn.11-16) as long as the (fragmentary?) seal impressions remain unpublished.

[11] Borger (1967:564) translates "Schenkungsurkunde" instead of votive seal. The seal of Uṣur-amassu also figures in Smith 1926; cf. Goff 1956:30f. = 1963:203.

[12] Why most English versions translate "as a seal" is not clear to me.

[13] It may be noted here that seals have never appeared in Mesopotamian foundation deposits to date.

contest scenes (Rathje 1977). It may well be, then, that in the Song of Songs, the beloved seeks, not only the physical intimacy noted above, but the status-symbol function assumed by the seal in burials: even as the latter perpetuates the owner's standing in death, so the beloved declares that her lover's role with regard to her will outlive him.

In Mesopotamian lore, however, seals were not only an accompaniment to death but even, at times, its cause. We therefore turn to yet another role played by these tiny objects, namely that of seals as weapons.

Our initial and somewhat ambiguous sources for this apparently incongruous role are mythological. In the fragmentary myth of "the slaying of Labbu," an unknown deity is instructed to hold (?) his votive seal (Goff 1956:35f. = 1963:208; cf. Hallo 1962:14 n. 107)[14] or perhaps "the seal at your throat (so CADK 544c; cf. CADN 1:303b) before your face" and thus defeats this mythological beast. And in the "Etiological myth of the 'seven sages'" (Reiner 1961) which is now known to form part of the third tablet (chapter) of the ritual enclosure series (bīt mēsiri; Borger 1974), the fourth of these antediluvian sages (Piriggal-abzu) is described as one who hung his seal on the goat-fish sacred to Ea, lord of the watery depths, and so angered that deity there that the latter either "cut(?) the cords from(?) the seal around his neck(?)" (Reiner 1961:5 n.1) or "killed (him) with the seal around his neck" (CADN 1:303b) or else that "a fuller killed him with his own seal" (Borger 1974:192).

But a clearer image once more emerges from the Babylonian omen literature. Three times, the so-called historical omens tell us, a reigning monarch was assassinated by the seals of his courtiers. Rimush, probably Manishtushu, and also Sharkalisharri, all of the great Sargonic dynasty, are all said to have met this fate. The modern explanations offered for this persistent tradition have diverged widely. One theory has it that it was the magical potency of the seals that lent them their power (Goff 1956:36f. = 1963:208f.).[15] Others replace "seal" by "stylus" or "heavy stone tablet" in the translation or suggest some other cylindrically shaped object or even a sealed (and perhaps forged) document (for all these theories see Wiseman 1974:254). A third approach simply rejects the whole genre of "historical" omens as devoid of historical fact (Cooper 1981; cf. Reiner 1974). However, not only has recent research vindicated some of these omens (Hallo 1978; cf. Starr 1977) but, already in 1929, Gadd (1929:96, cited Goff 1956:37 n.3 = 1963:209 n.76) had suggested that the copper clothing pins of Ur in Early Dynastic III times (see above) could have done the deed. From here it is only a short step to the later pin-mounts. While these were occasionally perhaps of gold or silver, especially where a divine or royal owner was involved (e.g., Franke 1977: 63f.), the servants of the king would make do with a wooden one,[16] and this could be sharpened to a deadly point! Thus the courtiers could come into the royal presence, ostensibly unarmed, but at a signal whip the necklaces from their necks and plunge the sharpened seal-mounts into their unsuspecting victim (Hallo, 1962:14 n.107; cf. Hirsch 1963:13 n.128).

While the Bible has no exact parallel, I invite you to consider the case of the left-handed judge Ehud, who rid Israel of its Moabite oppressor with a well-timed thrust from the dagger concealed on his right side under his cloak (Judges 3:15-end). And, in fact, we do

---

[14] Literally "the seal of your life."

[15] Goff's treatment is in the context of a larger study of "cylinder seals as amulets" (1956:23-37 = 1963:195-210), a role not dealt with here.

[16] Note the equation ^{giš}bulug = palukku in Landsberger, MSL 6:33:313.

have a possible analogue to the proposed configuration of cylinder-seal, pin-mount and necklace attachment in the Biblical passage with which we began. For there has never been a wholly satisfactory explanation for the particular, not to say peculiar, combination of personal effects demanded of Judah as his pledge. His seal—yes—was clearly distinctive and identifiable. But why cord and staff? How would anyone, even their owner, tell them apart? Already Moscati realized that the cord must be the necklace by which the seal was worn—and that the seal must therefore have been a cylinder seal (1949:316f.; followed by Speiser and other commentators). Then why not take matters one step further and suppose that the staff (*maṭṭeh*) was the pin on which the cylinder seal was mounted?[17]

If, then, we can assume the existence of the cylinder-seal in the purview and imagery of the Biblical author, we may now turn to its ultimate metaphoric role: as the symbol of completion, perfection, infinity. These qualities seem inexplicable in the stamp seal, which, if one may borrow a linguistic concept, is the very essence of the "punctual." The stamp seal is impressed once and for all and its impression is framed in a finite space. But the cylinder seal is quintessentially "durative." It is round and its impression is essentially endless—or rather, it need end only where the impressed surface ends. Hence it conjures up not only the image of legal perfection as in concluding agreements, but of perfection generally. It is in this sense that Ezekiel begins his description of the King of Tyre: "You were the seal of perfection, full of wisdom and flawless in beauty, you were in Eden, the garden of God" (28:12b-13a).

And again, the royal focus of the Near Eastern matrix gives way to the divine preoccupation of the Israelite world-view, the royal seal to the divine seal. If I may once more quote Franz Rosenzweig, who entitled the third and final book of the third and final part of the Star of Redemption, "The Star or the Eternal Truth," he began that book thus: "God is truth. Truth is his signet. By it he is known" (1972:380). Or as it is phrased in the Talmudic passage to which he was alluding: "The seal of the Holy One Blessed be He is truth" (Shabbat 55a; Sanhedrin 64a etc.).

Beyond this I would be foolhardy to try to take matters. The seal as metaphor for baptism in the New Testament and for many other referents in classical antiquity was exhaustively and definitively dealt with by Dölger more than seventy years ago. I leave it to others to evaluate this evidence.

Bibliography

Aharoni, Yohanan, ed.
  1973 "Beer-Sheba I, Excavations at Tel Beer-Sheeba, 1969-1971 seasons," (Tel Aviv University, Institute of Archaeology).
Benito, Carlos A.
  1969 "Enki and Ninmah and Enki and the World Order" Ph.D. Thesis, U. of Pennsylvania.
Borger, Rykle
  1967 *Handbuch der Keilschriftliteratur*, Band I, Repertorium der Sumerischen und Akkadischen Texte (Berlin, Walter de Gruyter and Co.).
  1974 "Die Beschwörungsserie *bīt mēseri* und die Himmelfahrt Henochs," *JNES* 33:183-196.
Bottéro, Jean
  1949 "Les inventaires de Qatna," *RA* 43:1-40, 137-215.

---

[17]Note however that seal and staff are combined in Egyptian investitures dated to Sesostris I and Rameses II (Schott 1957:181f.).

Boyer, Georges
  1939 "'Son ongle en guise de sceau'," *Symbolae . . . Paulo Koschaker Dedicatae* (= Studia et Documenta 2) 208-218, reprinted in *Mélanges d'histoire du Droit Oriental* (1965) 3-13.
Brinkman, J. A.
  1968 *A Political History of Post-Kassite Babylonia* (= An.Or. 43).
Buchanan, Briggs
  1967 "The prehistoric stamp seal: a reconsideration of some old excavations," *JAOS* 87:265-279, 525-540.
  1981 *Early Near Eastern Seals in the Yale Babylonian Collection* (New Haven and London, Yale U.P.).
Cooper, Jerrold
  1980 "Apodotic death and the historicity of 'Historical' omens" *RAI* 26:*Death in Mesopotamia*, ed., B. Alster (= Mesopotamia 8) 99-105.
Deimel, Anton
  1928- *Šumerisches Lexikon* II. Teil (Rome, Pontifical Biblical Institute).
   33
Dölger, F. I.
  1911 *Sphragis: eine altchristliche Taufbezeichnung in ihren Beziehungen zur profanen und religiösen Kultur des Altertums* (= Studien zur Geschichte und Kultur des Altertums V 3-4).
Falkenstein, Adam
  1936 *Archaische Texte aus Uruk* (= Ausgrabungen der Deutschen Forschungsgemeinschaft in Uruk-Warka 2).
  1959 "Zwei Rituale aus seleukidischer Zeit," *UVB* 15:36-44.
  1964 "Sumerische religiöse Texte," *ZA* 56:4-129.
Friedrich, Johannes
  1952 *Hethitisches Wörterbuch* (Heidelberg, Carl Winter).
Gelb, I. J.
  1977 "Typology of Mesopotamian seal inscriptions," in Gibson and Biggs: 107-126.
Gibson, McGuire and Robert D. Biggs
  1977 *Seals and Sealing in the Ancient Near East* (= Bibliotheca Mesopotamia 6).
Gluck, J., ed.
  1974 New Studies 1960-1973 in Memoriam Arthur Upham Pope (= *A Survey of Persian Art: From Prehistoric Times to the Present*, 15).
Goff, Beatrice L.
  1956 "The rôle of amulets in Mesopotamian Ritual Texts" *The Journal of the Warburg and Courtauld Institutes*, vol. 19, 1-39.
  1963 *Symbols of Prehistoric Mesopotamia* (New Haven and London, Yale U.P.).
Hallo, William W.
  1962 "The royal inscriptions of Ur: a typology," *HUCA* 33:1-43.
  1964 "The road to Emar," *JCS* 18:57-88.
  1967 Review of RLA 3/1, *JAOS* 87:62-66.
  1970 "The cultic setting of Sumerian poetry," *RAI* 17:116-134.
  1977 "Seals lost and found," in Gibson and Biggs 1977 55-60; "Correction to *Seals Lost and Found*,
  & 1981   BM 6 (1977), 55f." *RA* 75:95.
  1981 Review of Cooper, *The Return of Ninurta to Nippur*, *JAOS* 101:253-257.
  1981 "Introduction," in Briggs Buchanan, *Early Near Eastern Seals in the Yale Babylonian Collection*. pp. ix-xv. "Seal Inscriptions," *Ibid.*, 440-468.
  1983 "Cult statue and divine image: a preliminary study" in Hallo, Moyer, and Perdue, *Scripture in Context* 2: *More Essays on the Comparative Method* (Winona Lake, Ind., Eisenbrauns).
Hirsch, Hans
  1963 "Die Inschriften der Könige von Agade," *AfO* 20:1-82.

Jacobsen, Thorkild
    1953   "The Reign of Ibbī-Suen," *JCS* 7:36-47.
    1980   "Death in Mesopotamia (abstract)," *RAI* 26 (= Mesopotamia 8) 19-24.
Joannès, F.
    1980   "Kaššaia, fille de Nabuchodonosor II," *RA* 74:183.
Kingsbury, Edwin C.
    1967   "He set Ephraim before Manasseh," *HUCA* 38:129-136.
Kramer, Samuel Noah
    1967   "Ur-Nammu's death and burial," *JCS* 21:104-122.
Krecher, Joachim
    1966   *Sumerische Kultlyrik* (Wiesbaden, Harrassowitz).
Lambdin, Thomas O.
    1953   "Egyptian loan words in the Old Testament," *JAOS* 73:145-155.
Landsberger, Benno
    1967   *MSL* 9.
Leemans, W. F.
    1952   *Ishtar of Lagaba and her Dress* (Studia . . . de Liagre Böhl 1/1).
    1960   *Legal and Administrative Documents* . . . (= Studia . . . de Liagre Böhl 1/3).
Levine, Baruch A.
    1968   "*Mulūgu/Melûg*: the origins of a Talmudic legal institution," *JAOS* 88:271-285.
Loding, Darlene
    1974   "A Craft Archive from Ur" Ph. D. Thesis, U. of Pennsylvania.
    1976   *Economic Texts from the Third Dynasty* (= *UET* 9).
Mallowan, Max E. L.
    1950   "The excavations at Nimrud (Kalhu), 1949-1950," *Iraq* 12:147-183.
Milgrom, Jacob
    1981   "The Tassel and the Tallith," (= The Fourth Annual Rabbi Louis Feinberg Memorial Lecture in Judaic Studies, pp. 1-9).
Moscati, Sabatino
    1949   "I sigilli nell'Antico Testamento: studio esegetico-filologico," *Biblica* 30:314-338.
Muhly, James D.
    1981   Review of Gibson and Biggs 1977, *JAOS* 101:399-401.
Oberhuber, Karl
    1972   *Die Kultur des Alten Orients* (= Handbuch der Kulturgeschichte, 2. Abteilung, ed. E. Thurnher).
Opificius, Ruth M.
    1971   "Gottessiegel," *Reallexikon der Assyriologie* 3:576-580.
Oppenheim, A. Leo
    1974   "A new Cambyses incident," in Gluck, pp. 3497-3502.
Owen, David I.
    1975   *The John Frederick Lewis Collection,* (= Materiali per il Vocabolario Neosumerico 3).
Pettinato, Giovanni
    1982   *Testi Lessicali Bilingui della Bibliotheca L. 2769* (= Materiali Epigrafici di Ebla 4).
Pohl, A.
    1951   "Personalnachrichten," *Or.* 20:254.
    1954   "Assyriologische Rundschau. 3," *Or.* 23:181-187, with: review of Leemans, *Ishtar of Lagaba and Her Dress, Ibid.* 23:181.
Pope, Marvin H.
    1977   *The Anchor Bible : Job* (Garden City, Doubleday).
Porada, Edith and Farai Basmachi
    1951   "Nergal in the Old Babylonian Period," *Sumer* 7:66-68.

Porada, Edith
  1965   "The relative chronology of Mesopotamia. Part I. Seals and Trade (6000-1600 B.C.)," in Robert
            W. Ehrich, ed., *Chronologies in Old World Archaeology* (Chicago U.P.).
Rainey, Anson F.
  1973   "The cuneiform inscription on a votive cylinder from Beer Sheba," in Aharoni 1973:61-70.
Rathje, William L.
  1977   "New tricks for old seals: a progress report," in Gibson and Biggs, 25-32.
Reiner, Erica
  1961   "The etiological myth of the 'seven sages'," *Or.* 30:1-11.
  1974   "New light on some historical omens," Güterbock AV (= Anatolian Studies, Nederlands Insti-
            tuut Istanbul 35:257-261.
Renger, Johannes
  1977   "Legal aspects of sealings in ancient Mesopotamia," in Gibson and Biggs 1977:75-88.
Römer, W. H. Ph.
  1978   Review of D. I. Owen, *The John Frederick Lewis Collection,* (= Materiali per il Vocabulario
            Neosumerico 3) in *BiOr* 35:188-191.
Rössler, Otto
  1952   "Der semitische Charakter der libyschen Sprache," *ZA* 50:121-150.
Root, Margaret Cool
  1982   Review of Gibson and Biggs 1977, *JNES* 41:58-60.
Rosenzweig, Franz
  1972   *The Star of Redemption* translated by William W. Hallo (Boston, Beacon Press).
Rost, Paul
  1893   *Die Keilschrifttexte Tiglat-Pilesers III* (Leipzig, E. Pfeiffer).
Roth, Martha Tobi
  1979   "Scholastic Tradition and Mesopotamian Law: A Study of FLP 1287, A Prism in the Collection
            of the Free Library of Philadelphia," Ph.D. Thesis, U. of Pennsylvania.
Salonen, Armas
  1968   "Zum Aufbau der Substrate im Sumerischen," *Studia Orientalia* 38:3-12.
  1969   *Die Fussbekleidung der alten Mesopotamier* (= Annales Academiae Scientiarum Fennicae B 157).
  1972   *Die Ziegeleien im alten Mesopotamien* (= Annales Academiae Scientiarum Fennicae B 171).
Schneider, Nikolaus
  1947   "Stellvertretende Siegelung der Vertragsurkunden in der Ur III-Zeit," *Or.* 16:417-421.
Schott, Siegfried
  1957   "Wörter für Rollsiegel und Ring," *Wiener Zeitschrift für die Kunde des Morgenlandes* 54:177-
            185 (= H. Junker AV).
Skaist, Aaron
  1980   "The background of the Talmudic formula WHKL ŠRYR WQYM," *Studies in Hebrew and
            Semitic Languages* (Bar-Ilan U.P.) xl-liv.
Smith, Sydney
  1926   "Assyriological notes: the seal before the god," *JRAS* 1926; 442-446.
Starr, Ivan
  1977   "Notes on some published and unpublished historical omens," *JCS* 29:157-166.
Stephens, Ferris J.
  1931   "The ancient significance of ṣîṣît," *Journal of Biblical Literature* 50:59-70.
Strommenger, Eva
  1971   "Grabbeigabe I. Irak und Iran," *Reallexikon der Assyriologie* 3:605-608.
Wiseman, D. J.
  1974   "Murder in Mesopotamia," *Iraq* 36:249-260.

ERRATA: Plate XII-1, line 2 should be (ca. 2500 B.C.) not (ca. 2800 B.C.)

THE SNAKE AND THE TREE IN THE ICONOGRAPHY
AND TEXTS OF SYRIA DURING THE BRONZE AGE*

ELIZABETH WILLIAMS-FORTE

University of California, Berkeley

In Genesis III:1-24, the snake and the tree (Pl. I-1) have frequently been associated with lingering influence of earlier Canaanite cult and practice upon the peoples of ancient Israel. The serpent has been variously identified with the major gods of the earlier inhabitants of these regions, either El, the head of the Ugaritic pantheon, or Baal, the storm god.[1] The tree, on the other hand, has been associated with the sacredness of vegetation in the form of the asherah venerated by the peoples of Syria-Palestine prior to the arrival of the Israelites.[2] The intention of this paper is to discuss a series of pictorial representations of the storm god on artifacts from sites in Syria-Palestine and Anatolia which provide detailed evidence of the close association of this god, generally identified as Baal/Hadad, with the serpent and with a tree during the Middle Bronze Age (ca. 2000-1600 B.C.).

On the whole, the serpent in pre-Biblical art and texts of these regions has been considered a sea monster making its relationship to the serpent in the garden in the later biblical

*This article is derived from a portion of the author's doctoral dissertation defended in Spring 1982 at Columbia University. "Mythic Cycles: The Iconography of the Gods of Water and Weather in Syria and Anatolia during the Middle Bronze Age (ca. 2000-1600 B.C.)." The research and writing of this dissertation were generously supported by a Columbia University Travel Grant and by the Lane Cooper Foundation.

For his help and kindness during my months of research at the Louvre and for permission to incorporate an unpublished Louvre seal in this article, I would especially like to thank M. Pierre Amiet, curateur-en-chef of the Départment des Antiquités Orientales at the Musée du Louvre. Similar help was given me by M. Raoul Curiel, curator of the Cabinet des Médailles of the Bibliothèque Nationale, who has generously granted me permission on behalf of the Seyrig family to publish several seals from the collection of M. Henri Seyrig, a kindness I gratefully acknowledge here. I should also like to thank Edith Porada, Emeritus Professor of Ancient Near Eastern Art History and Archaeology at Columbia University, for allowing me to include a drawing of a British Museum seal which will appear in her forthcoming monograph on the Syrian seals in the collection of that museum, and Mme. Irène Aghion of the Bibliothèque Nationale and M. Dominique Beyer of the Musée du Louvre for their help with the illustrations. Corethia Qualls, Paula Spilner, Joseph Forte, and Julia Asher-Greve have contributed to the formulation of the ideas presented in this article through conversations and encouragement.

[1] See H. Ringgren, *Israelite Religion*, tr. David Green (London, 1966), 111 and 37; F. Hvidberg, "The Canaanite Background of Gen. I-III," *Vetus Testamentum* 10/3 (1960), 285-294; N. Wyatt, "Interpreting the Creation and Fall Story in Genesis 2-3," *ZAW* 93 (1981), 10-21; and for Wyatt's interpretation of the serpent as the Ugaritic god Athtar, "'Attar and the Devil," *Glasgow University Oriental Society Transactions* 25 (1973/74), 85-97.

[2] H. Ringgren, *Israelite Religion*, 24-25 and 157-158; N. Wyatt, *ZAW* 93 (1981), 17. For the asherah in general, see: W. L. Reed, *The Asherah in the Old Testament*, 1949; W. L. Reed, "Asherah," in *Interpreter's Dictionary of the Bible*, A-D, (1962), 250-252.

imagery seem unlikely.[3] However, the characteristics of the serpent and the storm god who battles and conquers this creature in the earlier art of the lands of the Bible seem to suggest the snake's association not with the sea, but with the powers of dark earth, namely the underworld, and with infertility. An epic combat between the forces of life and fertility, embodied by the storm god and his tree weapon, and the embodiment of death and sterility, the snake, seem to be portrayed, perhaps providing the background for the association of the serpent with the tree and with the symbolic "death" of mankind in Genesis III.

Before proceeding further to a discussion of the scenes depicting the storm god's battle with a serpent, his victory over it with a tree weapon, and his subsequent worship by human and divine figures, it is necessary to discuss the identifying characteristics of the weather god, past identifications of this god in the art and texts of these regions, and the geographical distribution of the artifacts bearing images of this god and of his battle with a serpent. Rather than multiple gods of weather of distinctly Anatolian or Syrian nature, there appears to be a single, vigorous, young weapon-wielding storm god identifiable by his attributes (the bull, the mountains, and the snake) and, most critically, by his actions or battles, on artifacts from each of these regions. Despite readily apparent differences in style, the iconography of the storm god in Anatolia and Syria during the first half of the second millennium B.C. is virtually identical and focuses on the attributes of this deity, which define his nature, and which appear to have been conquered by the god. Thorkild Jacobsen considers the earliest non-anthropomorphic and later anthropomorphic shapes of a god to be involved in a protracted contest in which the non-human form becomes the enemy of the god.[4] This model, positing a cycle that involves the transition from non-human to human deities and their combat, may be applicable to the Anatolian and Syrian weather god who appears to battle and conquer his attributes, among them, the serpent.

The anthropomorphic god associated with the bull, with mountains and with the branching lightning, in the art of the first half of the second millennium B.C. in Syria and Anatolia has been identified as a weather or storm god indigenous to these regions since at least the early twentieth century. The first systematic study devoted entirely to the iconography of the weather on the bull was undertaken by Halil Demiricioğlu. Tracing the imagery of the bull and the god in later Roman art (Jupiter Dolichenus) to the Cappadocian seals of Anatolia in the early second millennium B.C., Demiricioğlu suggested that this deity originated in the regions of Anatolia and Syria.[5]

Most recently, A. Vanel devoted a monograph to the iconography of the storm god, basing the chronological development of the deity's imagery primarily on stratified artifacts

---

[3] See below pp. 00-00. In a discussion of the appearance of the serpent and of evil in the world in Genesis III.1, U. Cassuto reasons that "it was only to be expected that the theme (of evil) should be linked with one of the usual and well-known symbols connected therewith, and particularly with the ordinary *serpent*, an animal that is found in the sea and the rivers and on land, for the *dragons* and big serpents called *Leviathan* exist only in the sea, and could not appear in the garden." *A Commentary on the Book of Genesis* part 1, tr. Israel Abrahams (Jerusalem, 1961), 141.

[4] T. Jacobsen, *Toward the Image of Tammuz and other Essays on Mesopotamian History and Culture*, (Cambridge, Mass., 1970), 4 and 339, n.7; and T. Jacobsen, *The Treasures of Darkness: A History of Mesopotamian Religion* (New Haven, 1976), 128-130.

[5] H. Demircioğlu, *Der Gott auf dem Stier: Geschichte eines religiosen Bildtypus* (Berlin, 1939); I would like to thank Nimet Özgüç for having drawn my attention to this reference. For earlier identifications of this god, see: W. Ward, *The Cylinder Seals of Western Asia*, (Washington, D.C., 1910), 270-291; G. Contenau, *La glyptique Syro-Hittite*, (Paris, 1922).

that had appeared since Demiricioğlu's study, such as the artifactual material from the north Syrian site of Mari and from the earliest Kültepe/Kanesh excavation report. Vanel's study was the first to characterize systematically the physical appearance and attributes of the weather god on Anatolian and Syrian artifacts and to note the similarities that occur in the art of these two regions.[6]

Since Vanel's 1965 study of the weather god, critical new evidence for an evaluation of the nature of the weather god and of the chronological development of his imagery within the regions of Anatolia and Syria has appeared in the publication by Nimet Özgüç of the seals and seal impressions from Kültepe/Kanesh Karum level II and Ib and Acemhöyük[7] in central Anatolia, by Dominique Collon of the seals and seal impressions from Tell Atchana/Alalakh[8] in the Amuq region of southwestern Turkey, and by Thomas Beran of the seals and impressions from Boğazköy/Hattuša.[9] The publication of the seals and impressions from these important sites in Anatolia and Syria significantly increases the amount of material upon which to base a study of the development of the iconography of the weather god during the Bronze Age while at the same time attesting to the very similar nature of the god of storm appearing in the pictorial representations of these two regions.

In an article dealing with the later form of the storm god, the "smiting" god who appears on artifacts of eighteenth to seventeenth century date in Anatolia and Syria, Collon pointed out similarities in the representation of the god in these regions and identified him as the weather god mentioned in texts—Adad, Hadad, Teshub or Baal—on the basis of his pose and attributes.[10] As Collon noted, previous identification of the weather god with deities mentioned in texts from the regions of Syria and Anatolia have almost universally equated this god with either the West Semitic/Ugaritic god Baal/Hadad or the Hurrian/Hittite god, Teshub. Baal/Hadad and Teshub are generally considered as names for the same divine being ^{d}IM or ^{d}U, whose powers involve storms, lightning and fertilizing rain.[11]

Later Hittite Empire texts which describe images of the weather god worshipped at

[6] A. Vanel, *L'Iconographie du dieu de l'orage*, Cahiers de la Revue Biblique 3 (Paris, 1965).

[7] For *Karum* level II, see: N. Özgüç, *The Anatolian Group of Cylinder Seal Impressions from Kültepe*, Türk Tarih Kurumu Yayınlarından, 5 serie, 22 (Ankara, 1965). For level Ib, see: N. Özgüç, *Seals and Seal Impressions of Level Ib from Karum Kanish*, Türk Tarih Kurumu Yayınlarından, 5 Seri. Sa. 25 (Ankara, 1968). For Acemhöyük, see N. Özgüç, "Acemhöyük Saraylarında bulunmuş olan Muhur Bakıları," *Belleten* 41:162 (1977 357-381; N. Özgüç, "Seals Impressions from the Palaces at Acemhöyük," in *Ancient Art in Seals*, ed. E. Porada (Princeton, 1980), 61-101.

[8] D. Collon, *The Seal Impressions from Tell Atchana/Alalakh*, Alter Orient und Altes Testament 27 (Neukirchen-Vluyn, 1975); D. Collon, *The Alalakh Cylinder Seals*, BAR International Series 132 (London, 1982).

[9] T. Beran, *Die hethitische Glyptik von Boğazköy I. Die Siegel und Siegelabdrucke der vor-und-althethitischen Grosskönige*, WVDOG, 76 (Berlin, 1967). For the Late Bronze Age, see the important material from Meskéné/Emar: D. Beyer, "Notes préliminaires sur les empreintes de sceaux de Meskéné, in *Actes du Colloque de Strasbourg. Le Moyen-Euphrate, zone de contacts et d'échanges* (Strasbourg, 1980), 265-283; D. Beyer, "Les empreintes de sceaux," in *Meskéné-Emar: Dix ans de travaux 1972-1982*, ed. D. Beyer (Paris, 1982), 61-68.

[10] D. Collon, "The Smiting God: A Study of a Bronze in in the Pomerance Collection in New York," *Levant* 4 (1972), 111-135.

[11] *Ibid.*, 111ff.; D. Collon, *Seal Impressions from Alalakh*, p. 184. And also see: W. Helck, *Betrachtungen zur grossen Göttin und dem ihr verbundenen Göttheiten*, Religion und Kultur des Alten Mittelmeerwelt in Parallel Forschungen II, (Munich and Vienna, 1971), 95-96; A. Kapelrud, *Ba'al in the Ras Shamra Texts*, (Copenhagen, 1952), 37-39 and 43-51; M. J. Dahood, "Ancient Semitic Deities in Syria and Palestine," in *Le Antiche Divinità Semitiche* (Studi Semitici I) (Rome, 1958), 75-79.

different cult centers have been used as evidence for the existence of a multiplicity of gods of storm.[12] However, these lists designate the weather god by the same ideogram ^dU and differentiate the images according to provenance and material (silver, bronze, wood) and to whether it is in bull or anthropomorphic form but rarely distinguish them by attributes.[13] In a discussion of Hittite texts mentioning "all of the storm gods" or "all the Ishtars," Maurice Viéyra maintains that each of the gods must participate in the same nature, for "*mutatis mutandis*, le phénomène est le même qui fait que la Vièrge de Fatima est et n'est pas la Vièrge de Lorette."[14] Similar lists of "Adads" and "Baals" occur in Mesopotamian and Syrian texts and are understood as designating the same god worshipped at different sanctuaries.[15] Thus, although later Hittite texts describe images of the weather god at different cult centers such as Arinna and Nerik, the god may represent essentially the same god, perhaps with regional differentiations, but on the whole with similar attributes.

The earliest known images of an indigenous Anatolian and Syrian god of weather occur in the *karum* or trading post at Kültepe, ancient Kanesh, level II, ca. 1920-1840 B.C.[16] Mellink has stated that here these gods appear "all of a sudden and full-fledged in the designs of the cylinder seals.[17] Considering the fragmentary state of our knowledge of the region in this period, however, the uniqueness of the Kültepe evidence may be more apparent than real. The significance of Kültepe for our knowledge of the storm god may lie not in its singularity, but in its apparent role as a point of contact between a wide variety of peoples and traditions of different regional origin. In the late nineteenth to eighteenth century B.C., artifacts representing the weather god are distributed over a much broader area at sites in several principal regions of Anatolia and Syria: at Kültepe/Kanesh *Karum* Ib; Acemhöyük near Aksaray and Karahoyük near Konya in central Anatolia, at the inland Syrian site of Tell Mardikh/Ebla; the coastal site of Byblos, the Middle Euphrates site of Mari; and at the slightly later Tell Atchana/Alalakh in the Amuq Region.[18] This geographical distribution

[12] For example, see: N. Özgüç, *The Anatolian Group*, 65.

[13] See L. Jacob-Rost, "Zu den Hethitischen Bildbeschreibungen," *MIO*, vols. 8:2 and 9 (1961), 161-217 and 175-239, esp. 204-209.

[14] M. Viéyra, "Les textes hittites," in R. Labat, *et. al.*, *Les Religions du Proche Orient*, (Paris, 1970), 500.

[15] M. Pope, "Syrien: Die Mythologie der Ugariter und Phönizier," in *Götter und Mythen im Vorderen Orient. Die alten Kulturvölkes. I: Wörterbuch der Mythologie*, 1 (Berlin, 1965), 217-234; M. Astour, "Two Ugaritic Serpent Charms," *JNES* 27 (1968), 20.

[16] For the dating of *Karum* Kanesh, see: K. Balkan, *Observations on the Chronological Problems of Karum Kaniš*, Türk Tarıh Kurumu Yayınlarından, Ser. VII, no. 28 (Ankara, 1955); 46-59, esp. 45-47; L. L. Orlin, *Assyrian Colonies in Cappadocia*, Studies in Ancient History, 1, (The Hague, 1970), 208; M. T. Larsen, *The Old Assyrian City-State and its Colonies*, Mesopotamia, 4 (Copenhagen, 1976), 80-84; J. Börker-Klähn, "Zur Datierung von Karum Kaniš II und Ib," *Istanbuler Mitteilungen* 19/20 (1969-70), 79-83.

[17] M. Mellink, "Anatolia: Old and New Perspectives," *American Philosophical Society, Proceedings* 110:2 (1966), 120.

[18] For Kültepe Ib, see: N. Özgüç, *Seals of Level Ib*, Pls. XXII-2, XIX-b, and XXV-2. For Acemhöyük, see: N. Özgüç in *Ancient Art in Seals*, ed. E. Porada, 61-86, Figs. III-15 and III-27. For Karahüyük, see: S. Alp, *Zylinder und Stempelsiegel aus Karahüyük bei Konya*, Türk Tarih Kurumu Yayınlarından, V. Serie, no. 26 (Ankara, 1968), Abb. 13. For Tell Mardikh, see: P. Matthiae, "Empreintes d'un cylindre paléosyrien de Tell Mardikh," *Syria* 46 (1969), 1-43, Pls. I-1 and I-2. For Byblos, see: M. Dunand, *Fouilles de Byblos 1926-1932*, Bibliothèque archéologique et historique 24 (Paris, 1937), no. 2030, and for the Middle

along the major routes connecting Anatolia and Syria is most likely attributable to a continuation of the trading and other cultural contacts between these regions evidenced by the earlier material from Kültepe level II.[19] The continued appearance of the storm god characterized in the same manner in each region may suggest an even closer similarity and perhaps homogeneity of religious beliefs, at least in relation to this particular deity, shared by the inhabitants of the regions of Anatolia and Syria.

Because the earliest evidence for the Anatolian and Syrian anthropomorphic god of weather is found only at Kültepe/Kanesh in central Anatolia, a brief discussion of the general context of this evidence is necessary to explain their appearance at this single site, to elucidate the similarities in their iconography, and to provide the background for their subsequent geographical distribution at later sites throughout the regions of Anatolia and Syria.

Kültepe lies nineteen kilometers northwest of Kayserı in east central Anatolia and eleven kilometers south of the southernmost point of Turkey's major river, the Kızılırmak, which follows a horseshoe shaped course of more than seven hundred kilometers across the Anatolian plateau.[20] Excavation at Kültepe, begun by Hrozný in a single season in 1925, and reinitiated by the Turkish Historical Society under the direction of Tahsin and Nimet Özgüç in 1948 and continuing to the present day, has revealed two principal areas of occupation: a large "city" mound (*hüyük*) with material remains from the Early Bronze Age through the Roman era, and, to the northeast, a flat terrace, first inhabited in the late third to early second millennium B.C. (levels IV and III).[21] In antiquity Kültepe owed its importance to its proximity to rich natural resources (metals, timber) and to its location at the center of a system of trade routes set up to exploit these riches and dominate the Taurus and Anti-Taurus mountains to the south and east.[22]

Kültepe's strategic location attracted a cosmopolitan population. Thousands of clay cuneiform tablets discovered at Kültepe level II (ca. 1920-1840 B.C.) record the transactions of Assyrian merchants from Ashur in northern Mesopotamia living at *Karum* Kanesh and

---

Bronze Age date of this bronze, see O. Negbi, *Canaanite Gods in Metal: An Archaeological Study of Ancient Syro-Palestinian Figurines*, Tel Aviv University, Institute of Archaeology, Publications, 5 (Tel Aviv, 1976), 32. For Mari, see: A. Parrot, *Mission archéologique de Mari II: Le Palais: Documents et Monuments*, Bibliothèque archéologique et historique 70 (Beirut, 1959), 212-213, Pls. XLIII-XLIV, Fig. 115; A. Parrot, *Mission archéologique de Mari II: Le Palais: Peintures*, Bibliothèque archéologique et historique, 69 (Beirut, 1958), 70-82, Pls. XVII-E. And also see: P. Amiet, Syria 37 (1960), 215-232, and esp. 220-221. For Tell Atchana, see, Collon, *Seal Impressions from Alalakh*, Pl. XXV, nos. 32, 33-39, 40, 42-45; Collon, *The Alalakh Cylinder Seals*, nos. 20-21.

[19] For discussions of the economy and the pattern of trade relationships during the Middle Bronze Age, see: J. D. Muhly, *Copper and Tin: The Distribution of Mineral Resources and the Nature of the Metals Trade during the Bronze Age*, Transactions of the Connecticut Academy of Arts and Sciences 43 (Hamden, Conn., 1971). Also see: P. Gerstenblith, "The Levant in the Middle Bronze Age I Period and its Connection with Mesopotamia and Anatolia: A Study of Trade and Settlement Patterns," Diss. Harvard, 1977.

[20] Orlin, *Assyrian Colonies in Cappadocia*, 35-36.

[21] *Ibid.*, 79; T. Özgüç, *Kültepe Kaniš: New Researches at the Center of the Assyrian Trade Colonies*, Türk Tarih Kurumu Yayınlarından 5 Serie, 19 (Ankara, 1959).

[22] See: Orlin, *Assyrian Colonies in Cappadocia*, 35-44. Also see, for present-day mineral sources in Turkey, C. W. Ryan, *A Guide to the Known Minerals of Turkey* (Ankara, 1960). For the routes through the Anti-Taurus and Amanus, see: U. B. Alkim "An Ancient Road System in the Southwestern Anti-Taurus," *Belleten*, 23 (1959), 59-73 and U. B. Alkim, "The Amanus Region in Turkey," *Archaeology*, 22 (1969) 280-289 and map on p. 281.

trading with colonies or stations established at other Anatolian and possibly North Syrian sites at the beginning of the second millennium B.C.[23] People of Syrian—namely West Semitic Amorites—and possibly Hurrian origin also are documented by the tablets as living or trading at Kültepe.[24] Alongside these peoples of various regional origin were the native population of Kültepe, composed of speakers of the "Hattic" or pre-Hittite language, called Hattians,[25] and peoples bearing Indo-European names and probably representing the predecessors of the later Hittites of the mid-second millennium B.C.[26]

Accordingly, seals and impressions of four basic styles have been distinguished by Nimet Özgüç on tablets from Kültepe *Karum* level II: Old Assyrian, Old Babylonian, Old Anatolian and Old Syrian.[27] It is in these seals and seal impressions on clay tablets and *bullae* that we find the earliest images of an indigenous type of Anatolian and Syrian anthropomorphic god of weather.[28] Despite these stylistic differences, however, the gods on Anatolian and Syrian examples are characterized by identical attributes and actions, and seem therefore to be closely related in nature and perhaps in identity.

N. Özgüç determined the characteristic features of the Anatolian style and iconography primarily on the basis of comparison with earlier traditions within Anatolia and their continuation in pictorial representations of the Hittites in the last second millennium B.C. at Boğazköy/Hattuša.[29] Among features considered Anatolian, perhaps the most important was the appearance of the first clearly anthropomorphic deities riding the animal attributes that may have symbolized these gods in earlier Anatolian art. Approximately one-fourth of the published impressions of Old Anatolian style represent one or more gods upon bulls and have been interpreted as depicting at least six indigenous types of weather god by N. Özgüç.[30]

The bull, appearing from the earliest periods in the pictorial imagery of Anatolia,[31] was considered the emblematic animal of the weather god primarily on the basis of later Hittite texts describing images of that god in bull form.[32] The association of the bull with the god

---

[23] Orlin, *Assyrian Colonies in Cappadocia*, 26-26; M. T. Larsen, *The Old Assyrian City-State*, 236-241 and 371.

[24] Larsen, *The Old Assyrian City-State*, 43-47. Also see: J. Lewy, "Amurritica," *HUCA* 32 (1961), 66-67.

[25] See: J. G. Macqueen, *The Hittites and their Contemporaries in Asia Minor* (Boulder, Colorado, 1975), 29-33; O. R. Gurney, *The Hittites* (Baltimore, 1969), 122; H. Lewy, "Anatolia in the Old Assyrian Period," *Cambridge Ancient History* I:2 (1971), 716-719.

[26] J. G. Macqueen, *The Hittites*, p. 32.

[27] See: N. Özgüç, *The Anatolian Group*, pp. 45ff.; T. and N. Özgüç, *Kültepe Kazısı Raporu 1949: Ausgrabungen in Kültepe*, Türk Tarih Kurumu Yayınlarından, V serie, 12 (Ankara, 1953), pp. 229ff.; N. Özgüç, *Seals of Level Ib*, 37ff.

[28] N. Özgüç, *The Anatolian Group*, 63-65.

[29] T. and N. Özgüç, *Kültepe 1949*, 236-242. Also see: N. Özgüç, *The Anatolian Group*.

[30] N. Özgüç, *The Anatolian Group*, 47, 63-64.

[31] Evidence for the hunting of wild cattle and for the pictorial representation of the bull exists from the earliest period in Anatolia. See the rock paintings and engravings of bulls from Beldibi (c), Kara 'In, and Ikuzu 'In cave shelter; J. Mellaart, *Earliest Civilizations of the Near East* (New York, 1965) Figs. 47-48; J. Mellaart, *The Neolithic of the Ancient Near East* (New York, 1975), 92, Fig. 42. For bull imagery at the sixth millennium B.C. site of Çatal Hüyük in central Anatolia, see: J. Mellaart, *Çatal Hüyük, A Neolithic Town in Anatolia* (New York, 1967), Figs. 14-15, Pls. 22-23, 28, 64 and 88-89. For the faunal remains, see: D. Perkins, "Fauna of Çatal Hüyük," *Science* 164 (1969), 277-179.

[32] C. G. Brandenstein, *Hethitische Götter nach Bildbeschreibungen in Keilschrifttexten*, Mitteilungen der Vorderasiatisch-Aegyptischen Gesellschaft, 46:2 (1943).

of storm may have been based at least partially on that fertile animal's role as the means of propagation and thus perpetuation of the herds.[33] The "propogating" powers of rain and storm may have been considered analogous to the potent and forceful nature of the bull.[34]

The appearance of gods riding on bulls in association with specific motifs, such as mountains, which continued as attributes of the storm god identified by his Hittite hieroglyphic sign in the Hurrian/Hittite religious procession on the rock relief at Yazılıkaya near Boğazköy led Nimet Özgüç to identify these deities as weather gods.[35] Other features appearing in association with the god on the bull on the Old Anatolian style seals from Kültepe level II, such as the zig-zag lightning or parallel lines "falling" from the border of the seal and probably symbolizing rain seemed to support his identification.[36]

Old Syrian style seals, distinguished by Özgüç based on criteria derived from comparison with artifacts from Syrian sites, also show a god associated with the bull and identified as a weather god.[37] The equally critical role of bulls in the economy and socio-religious preoccupations of the people of Syria is evidenced by faunal remains and pictorial representations from the earliest periods at sites like Tell Mureybet,[38] and by later textual references to a god in bull form from Ras Shamra/Ugarit on the Syrian coast.[39]

Previously unrecognized attributes of the weather god on Old Anatolian and Old Syrian style seals, the serpent and the vegetal, branch-like lightning (Figs. 1, 2) seemingly used as a weapon against this creature, are essential for our understanding of the nature of the storm god and the recognition of his varying portrayal on the seals from Kültepe. Rather than multiple gods of weather, there appears to be a single active, probably young, weapon-wielding god identified by attributes such as a snake and the bull which may represent his conquered foes.[40] A second god, riding upon a bull before the active weapon-bearing weather god on nine of the twenty impressions depicting the god of storm on Old Anatolian style seals from *karum* level II, appears to be characterized by none of the attributes of a god of weather other than the bull.[41] This god may represent a second god associated with the bull at Kültepe, but generally shown enthroned upon this creature. This is the god of flowing streams and fishes which represents earthly, as opposed to heavenly, waters.[42] He is portrayed as a god of higher status,—always riding before the young god in procession— but of a less active nature—always riding with flat feet upon his bull and never brandishing

[33] See: C.Reed, "The Pattern of Animal Domestication in the Prehistoric Near East," in *The Domestication and Exploitation of Plants and Animals*, eds. P. Ucko and G. Dimbley (Chicago and New York, 1969), 364-367 and 372-375.

[34] H. G. Güterbock, "Hittite Religion," in *Ancient Religions*, ed. Vergilius Ferm (New York, 1950), 87-89.

[35] See, N. Özgüç, *The Anatolian Group*, p. 65.

[36] *Ibid.*, pp. 63-65.

[37] See, N. Özgüç, *Kültepe 1949*, 234-236 and N. Özgüç, *Seals of Level Ib*, 53-57.

[38] For a summary, see: J. Mellaart, *The Neolithic of the Ancient Near East*, 45-47.

[39] For example: T. H. Gaster, *Thespis: Ritual, Myth and Drama in the Ancient Near East*, (New York, 1950), 122.

[40] See: P. Amiet, *Syria* 37 (1960), 215-232; *Idem.*, "Le Temple ailé," *RA* 54 (1960), *Idem.*, 1-10; "Un vase rituel Iranien," *Syria* 42 (1965), 235-251; A. Vanel, *L'Iconographie du dieu de l'orage*, 79-93.

[41] N. Özgüç, *The Anatolian Group*, nos. 19, 20, 26, 28, 64-65, 70-71, and p. 64 for Nimet Özgüç's type c weather god. For this deity alone on his bull, see nos. 11 and 56.

[42] For the bull, human-headed or natural, previously unrecognized as attributes of the god associated with fish, the goat-fish, or streams of flowing water, see: N. Özgüç, *The Anatolian Group*, 60, nos. 7, 24, 48, 75.

weapons. Other identifying motifs that suggest the nature of this god are the cup he holds up to a sun and moon crescent, a fish that swims about him in the field, and the nude hero with streams that kneels on his rein.[43] These features—high status, pacific nature, associations with the bull, cup, sun, moon-crescent, fish and nude hero with streams—also characterize the enthroned water god on seals of Old Anatolian style from Kültepe[44] and may point to the identification of this god with that deity riding on the bull. Supportive evidence for this identification may be provided by the fact that the enthroned water god never receives processions of more than one deity on a bull and that god is always clearly identifiable as the active god of storm by his attributes. Indeed, nine of the twenty Old Anatolian style seals depicting the weather god portray him in the position of a minor deity before or behind the enthroned water god,[45] while an additional nine portray him riding behind the god, here suggested to represent the water god, standing upon his own bull emblem.[46]

Thus, at the cosmopolitan trading center or *karum* of Kültepe, ancient Kanesh, during the late twentieth and nineteenth century B.C., seal impressions on tablets seem to provide evidence of a single god of weather worshipped by Anatolians and Syrians. Features that characterize the anthropomorphic weather god on these earliest examples, and which continue to characterize him on later eighteenth and seventeenth century B.C. examples produced within Anatolia and Syria are:

1. an active, standing posture with feet level or with one foot raised
2. a crown with long pigtail or plume and an open or short garment
3. weapons like the mace and the axe
4. the lightning as a branching spear-like weapon or standard apparently used as a weapon against a snake
5. attributes like the bull, the mountains, and the snake
6. a close association with the nude goddess and the water god

Seals of the twentieth to mid-nineteenth century B.C. make clear reference to the weather god's mastery of the snake he grasps by the head. Rather than a passive attribute serving as an identifying characteristic, the snake is revealed as a conquered foe of the god by the lightning-weapon that rises from its head and by the snake's pose: head held tightly in the grasp of the god, its serpentine body hangs limply at the god's side (Figs. 1, 2, 4). Only on later Middle Bronze Age scenes (ca. 1800-1600 B.C.), which are the focus of this paper, are four stages of a seemingly narrative cycle representing the battle of weather god and serpent, and its aftermath, depicted:

1. the god impaling, with the tree-weapon/lightning, the serpent which rises against him from beneath the mountains
2. the victorious storm god displaying the conquered serpent to a goddess

[43] Özgüç, *The Anatolian Group*, nos. 19-20, 21, 26, 28, 64-65, 70-71; for fish, see: nos. 65, 71; for nude hero with streams, no. 11; cf. the nude goddess standing on the rein of the storm god, nos. 70-71.

[44] The close association of the god of flowing, presumably earthly waters, with the bull and with the younger active god of storm seems to suggest the indigenous Anatolian origin of this water god. For an identification of the Syrian god of flowing water as a non-Mesopotamian type of water god and his close association with the storm god, see: P. Amiet, *Syria* 37 (1960), 215-223; A. Vanel, *L'Iconographie du dieu de l'orage*, esp. 81-82.

[45] See, N. Özgüç, *The Anatolian Group*, nos. 4, 7, 14, 18, 24, 27, 29-30 and 39.

[46] See, N. Özgüç, *The Anatolian Group*, nos. 19-21, 26, 28, 64-65, and 70-71.

3. the victorious god displaying to human or divine worshippers the weapon with which he slew the serpent

4. and finally, the worship of the emblem of the god's victory, i.e. the tree-weapon/lightning, by divine, human, and composite figures

Late Bronze Age examples rarely portray a battle with the serpent but continue to show the weather god in association with the emblem of his victory, the tree-weapon.[47]

The earliest representations of the weather god with the snake occur on Old Anatolian and Old Syrian style seal impressions from Kültepe *Karum* level II and portray his victory over that creature. Old Syrian style seals from Kültepe (Fig. 4) and from Acemhöyük level III, at least partially contemporary with Kültepe *Karum* level II,[48] show the weather god holding a snake down to his side while lifting a vegetal standard before a nude goddess. Snakes are grasped in an identical manner by the weather god on seals of Anatolian style from Kültepe *Karum* level II[49] (Fig. 1) and on a seal impression on a Cappadocian tablet in the British Museum (Fig. 2). On these seals, the snake issues from beneath the mountain upon which the god stands. From the head of the serpent rises a branch-like element, extending to the border of the seal and probably representing the god's lightning.[50]

On these seals, the branch-like lightning issuing from the clearly conquered snake's head is similar to the vegetation that grows alongside "cones" that rest on the backs of bulls supporting the weather god on other Old Anatolian style seals from Kültepe[51] (Fig. 3). Perhaps these represent trees "growing" from mountains, symbolized by the traditional triangular shape.[52] The vegetal weapon which "grows" alongside the mountain thus may be integrally connected to the "heights" in cone-like form which appear beneath the foot of the weather god as conqueror of the serpent on other seals (Figs. 1, 2). The tail of the snake issuing from beneath the "cones" on these examples may suggest that the god's serpentine foe is also associated with the mountains and may dwell beneath them.

On these seals, the locale of the battle between the weather god and the snake, the abode

[47] See especially the Old Hittite seals in: E. Uzunoğlu, "Die Abrollung eines hethitischen Siegels auf einem Pithos," *Istanbuler Mitteilungen* 29 (1979), 65-75, esp. Tf. 8-9, and Abb. 2-4. I owe this reference to J. V. Canby.

[48] For Old Syrian (Syrian Colonly Style) seals from Kültepe, see: T. and N. Özgüç, *Kültepe 1949*, no. 695. On an unpublished example of Old Syrian style from Kültepe kindly shown me by Nimet Özgüç, the weather god grasps a snake that issues from beneath a mountain upon which he stands. He holds a standard surmounted, not by wings, but by a large orb. For Acemhöyük, see: N. Özgüç in *Ancient Art in Seals*, ed. E. Porada, III-21. For the date of early level III Acemhöyük, see: "Excavations at Acemhöyuk," *Anadolu*, 10 (1966), 49-52 and for the lower limit of level III, N. Özgüç, in *Ancient Art in Seals*, ed. E. Porada, 78.

[49] For Old Anatolian style seals from Kültepe, see: N. Özgüç, *The Anatolian Group*, nos. 31 and 70. Also see: E. Porada, *Corpus of Ancient Near Eastern Seals in North American Collections: The Collection of the Pierpont Morgan Library*, Bollingen Series 14 (Washington D.C., 1948) no. 894.

[50] These two elements, branch and snake, were previously interpreted as a single piece of plant-like vegetation, see: N. Özgüç, *The Anatolian Group*, 63.

[51] See: N. Özgüç, *The Anatolian Group*, nos. 19, 21, 26, 28-30, 39, 64-65 and for this weather god type "e" (a typographical error in the text reads "c"), p. 64.

[52] The possibility that the cone on the back of the bull emblem of the god represented a mountain was suggested by Edith Porada who cited Hetty Goldman as having made a similar suggestion, see: E. Porada, "Les Cylindres de la Jarre Montet," *Syria* XLIII (1966), 246, n.2 and H. Goldman, "The Sandon Monument of Tarsus," *JAOS* 60 (1940), 549.

of the serpent itself, and the "natural habitat" of the god's tree-weapon may be visually suggested to lie in the mountains.

On seals of Old Anatolian and Old Syrian style from Kültepe level II and from Acem-höyük, the vegetal weapon appears in close association with "heavenly" symbols like wings, cloud-like forms, and rain. The branch-like form rising from the head of the serpent on Old Anatolian style seals reaches to the upper border of the scene from whence issues the "rain" that in its zig-zag pattern appears similar to the linearly rendered branches of the vegetal weapon (Figs. 1, 2). These two forms, the vegetal weapon and the zig-zag lines emerging from the "heavens" on either side of the weather god may represent manifestations of the storms of the god that plummet to the earth below, the rain and the branching lightning. Perhaps the mysterious flaming lightning created by the weather god was compared in ancient people's mythopoeic thought with a visually related but familiar earthly manifestation of that god's creative force, the branching tree.

The relationship between the vegetal weapon, perhaps symbolic of the lightning, and heavenly phenomena, such as the rain, is rendered more clearly on three Old Syrian style seals from Kültepe *Karum* level II. On one seal (Fig. 4) the weather god grasps a serpent and lifts a long staff-like object, composed of upwardly curling plant-like volutes that merge with an undulating element issuing from the border of the pictorial field. Other seals show a vegetal weapon or standard with curling volutes supporting a winged form[53] (Fig. 5). The amorphous form and the wings appearing above the vegetal standard and in association with the conquered snake suggest their association to the more linearly rendered rain on the seals of Old Anatolian style and to meterological phenomena responsible for fertility, like storm-clouds. The god's vegetal weapon would then refer as well to the lightning or thunderbolts that issue from the sky or clouds and strike the earth below as a weapon.

Although slightly later seals continue to show "victory" scenes similar to those on seals of Old Anatolian and Old Syrian style from Kültepe level II, the actual combat between the serpent and the god and the role played by the tree-lightning in this battle are depicted for the first time on later artifacts of ca. 1850-1650 B.C. date. In these later scenes, the weapon used by the god, the locale of the battle, as well as the comrades-in-arms of the god are clearly defined, providing evidence for the exact nature of the struggle of the god with the snake.

Among the numerous artifacts showing victory or battle with the serpent, only two are from stratified contexts. A seal impression from Kültepe *Karum* level Ib shows the weather god standing upon two bulls while holding a volute standard similar to those held by the weather god on Early Colony period seals of Old Anatolian and Old Syrian style (Fig. 6). Like the earlier standards, it appears in association with a snake. Rather than grasped in the hand of the god, now upraised in the smiting gesture that is typical of this deity during the eighteenth century,[54] the serpent rises from the leg of the god below the vegetal standard. The nude goddess appears directly across from the triumphant god, continuing the tradition begun earlier on seals of both Old Syrian and Old Anatolian style from Kültepe.

---

[53] Also see: T. and N. Özgüç, *Kültepe 1949*, no. 695. For a similar winged form, but in this case above the head of the storm god grasping the snake, see the Old Syrian seal: E. Williams-Forte, "Cylinder Seals of the Old Assyrian Colony Period," in *Ladders to Heaven: Art Treasures from Lands of the Bible*, ed. Oscar White Muscarella, exh. cat. Royal Ontario Museum (Toronto, 1981), 162, no. 129.

[54] For the diagnostic features characterizing the weather god on artifacts of eighteenth century B.C. date, see: Vanel, *L'Iconographie du dieu de l'orage*, 83, and Collon, *Levant*, 4 (1972), 111ff.

Although found in a secondary context in a much later Roman tomb at S. Felice near Vincinza, Italy, a second seal, now in the archaeological museum in Florence, shows the weather god, snake and tree and may be dated on stylistic grounds to the Syrian Middle Bronze Age (Fig. 7). As on seals from Kültepe level Ib (Fig. 6), the level of Zimrilim at Mari and the slightly later Alalakh level VII, the Syrian seal from Italy shows a roundly modelled god in smiting posture wearing the pointed helmet and short kilt that are diagnostic features for a date ca. 1800-1600 B.C.[55] Figure 7 shows a "victory scene" similar to those found on earlier seals from Kültepe. Rather than holding the snake down at his side, as on earlier examples, the god stands in smiting pose and extends the snake and the tree-weapon toward a goddess.

Most critical, however, for our understanding of these scenes of victory, to which we will return, are scenes such as those on seals now in the British Museum, the Louvre, and in the Seyrig Collection in the Bibliothèque Nationale in Paris (Figs. 8, 9, 10). While holding a mace uplifted ready to strike, the god thrusts a tree-like weapon into the serpent's open throat. The god thus slays the serpent that rises against him with what looks like a living tree used as a weapon. The tree-weapon that rises from the gullet of the vertically writhing snake appears to be identical to the branch that issues from the snake's head on seals of Anatolian style from Kültepe *Karum* level II. Several artifacts of probably eighteenth to seventeenth century B.C. date, such as the "Baal au foudre" stele from Ras Shamra/Ugarit, depict the spear-like base of the tree, clearly emphasizing the fact that this tree-lightning is a weapon in the arsenal of the weather god as warrior[56] (Fig. 18).

On the seal in the Seyrig Collection (Fig. 10) as well as on seals in The Metropolitan Museum of Art[57] in New York, the weather god battles the serpent while standing upon two mountains. Lying across the mountain beneath the god's foot, or emerging from its base writhes the serpent. The serpent's home may therefore be in the mountain or perhaps beneath its base, a suggestion supported by earlier seals from Kültepe (Figs. 1, 2) and from Acemhöyük[58] which show the snake issuing from beneath the mountains upon which the weather god stands. Thus the locale of the battle between the storm god and the serpent and the original abode of the snake appear to be integrally connected with the mountains. The mountains thus assume an extremely significant role in the weather god's struggle with the serpent. In the Near East, mountains are traditionally considered "cosmic," the bond between heaven and earth, where the divine becomes manifest.[59] The weather god's stance, either stepping up onto or standing firmly upon the mountains, may suggest that the god conquered first the heights and then the serpent. His victory over the snake and its domain below or in the mountain and over the heights themselves may imply power over both the cosmic and infernal sphere.

[55] *Ibid.*

[56] Although found in a fourteenth century B.C. level, this stele has been dated to ca. 1900-1750 B.C. by the excavator on the basis of the god's pose and garb, see: C. Schaeffer, *Ugaritica II*, Bibliothèque archéologique et historique, 47 (Beirut, 1949), 121-130, Pl. 23. And also, see: Vanel, *L'Iconographie du dieu de l'orage*, 82-84.

[57] See the Moore Collection seal, now in The Metropolitan Museum of Art: G. A. Eisen, *Ancient Oriental Cylinder and other Seals with a Description of the Collection of Mrs. William H. Moore*, Oriental Institute Publications, 47 (Chicago, 1940), no. 158. Also see: *MMA* no. 68.57.1.

[58] N. Özgüç, in *Ancient Art in Seals*, ed. E. Porada, III-21.

[59] R. Clifford, *The Cosmic Mountain in Canaan and the Old Testament*, Harvard Semitic Monographs, 4 (Cambridge, Mass., 1972), 1 and *passim*.

The results of the god's battle with the serpent are portrayed on "victory scenes" of three types: the first in which the weather god holds his conquered foe, the snake, by its head (Figs. 7, 11), the second in which the serpent rises from the leg of the god as a tame attribute (Pl. I-1, I-3) (Figs. 6, 13), and the third in which he rides upon the back of the living serpent as mount (Pls. I-2, I-3). As on the earlier victory scenes of twentieth to nineteenth century B.C. date, wings and heavenly imagery like orbs and moon crescents appear above and around the tree-lightning of the weather god on later scenes portraying the god's victory over the serpent. The fertility aspects of the scene are further emphasized, it seems, by the appearance of a goddess opening her garment to reveal her nudity in association with vegetation-like buds and bowers. In contrast, the goddess that appears in association with the battle never opens her garment and frequently flails weapons (Fig. 9).

A seal in the Yale Babylonian Collection (Fig. 13) shows the triumphant storm god, with the conquered serpent emerging from behind his leg as on the Kültepe Ib seal (Fig. 6). His tree lightning is held aloft beneath a winged disc, clearly symbolic of the heavenly source of the god's lightning weapon. This heavenly imagery of wings, undulating cloud-like forms, or rain never occurred in the actual battle scenes but only in scenes such as this after his victory over the serpent. Perhaps the snake is symbolic of forces antithetical to fertility such as drought and death. With the death of the serpent, fertility symbolized by the lightning (which is itself the "murder" weapon) and the rain it heralds, return to the earth below.

On the seal now in Florence discussed above and on a seal in the Morgan Library in New York, the weather god grasps the snake and the tree-weapon in the same outstretched hand (Figs. 7, 11). The Morgan Library seal shows the god standing upon mountains and grasping in the same hand with the snake and the tree the rein of a couchant bull. Upon the captive bull's back stands a nude goddess with open garment. Heavenly orbs and stars appear in the field between and around them. On this seal, the gods control over the bull, and, by extension, the goddess is clearly suggested by the rein held along with other victory emblems, the tree-weapon and the snake.[60] That this scene combines elements from several victorious battles undertaken by the weather god may be suggested by a scene on a seal in Munich (Fig. 12). Here the weather god kneels to shoot a bull above which hovers a nude goddess, lying horizontally to the bull. Directly behind the bull appear all the elements of the god's battle with the snake: the serpent itself, the tree-weapon, and a semi-clad goddess. Since the god's battle with a bull here appears alongside a snake from the head of which rises a tree-weapon, it may be suggested that the bull was conquered after the serpent. Thus, the appearance of a bull alongside mountains and the snake in the "victory scenes" of the twentieth to nineteenth centuries B.C. also may represent a composite imagery displaying all the conquered foes of the triumphant weather god.[61]

The third type of victory scene shows the conquered snake serving as the living mount of the weather god replacing the bull which is that god's most frequent mode of transport. On a seal in the Seyrig Collection in Paris (Pl. I-2), the weather god mounts a horned serpent and gestures with a tree-weapon and multiple mace toward a nude goddess. The nude goddess stands with hands cupping her breasts beneath a unique bower composed of petal-like vegetal forms. A second Seyrig Collection seal (Pl. I-3) shows the serpent, impaled by the tree-weapon held by the god, gliding toward a goddess. Here the goddess holds what has

---

[60] Amiet, *RA* 54 (1960), 8-9.

[61] This seal, as well as other composite scenes showing the conquered foes of the storm god (the nude "hero," the snake and the bull) will be discussed in a future article by the present author.

29

traditionally been interpreted as her open garment.[62] This garment ends in petal forms identical to those that appear on the skirt of the goddess revealing herself on the Morgan Library seal (Fig. 11). Thus, whereas the battle scenes occur in connection with a variety of goddesses, some with war-like characteristics, the victory scenes almost always take place before a goddess whose fertility aspect is emphasized through her nudity and her association with vegetation.

The third phase of the narrative sequence telling the story of the storm god's victory over the serpent portrays the worship of the god displaying the weapon used to kill the snake by human and divine figures (Fig. 1; Pl. II-4). In these scenes, the victorious deity displays the weapon with which he slew the serpent to human and divine worshippers rather than to the seemingly welcoming goddess of the victory scenes. Rather than providing literal evidence of the god's victory through showing both the snake and the murder weapon together in the god's hand, these scenes merely imply the successful completion of the battle by the weather god who grasps a tree-weapon or spear.

On a seal in the Louvre, the storm god holds the tree-lightning aloft above an offering table while a worshipper wearing kingly attire gestures reverentially toward the victorious deity (Fig. 14). Similarly, an offering table appears in another worship scene in the Seyrig Collection (Pl. II-4). On this seal, the god's tree-weapon appears as a standard with its base resting on the ground, recalling the earlier vegetal standards of the Kültepe level II seal impressions (Figs. 4, 5).

The worship scenes on this group of seals are closely related to the iconography of the "Baal au foudre" stele from Ras Shamra/Ugarit (Fig. 15). What interests us here, however, is the weapon held by the god on this stele. Traditionally interpreted as stylized lightning of the weather god,[63] this spear with branching shaft is clearly identical to the tree-weapon found on the seals. Below the point of the spear appear a series of undulating lines, symbolic either of rounded mountainous forms or of the writhing serpent. Standing on a podium before the god appears a female figure, probably a goddess, in a garment with rolled borders. An identical small podium supports the god's reined bull on a seal impression from Tell Mardikh/Ebla level IIIB (ca. 1800 B.C.) (Fig. 16). That the goddess is placed upon a dais identical to the bull's on the Ebla seal perhaps supports the god's suggested propriety relationship with the goddess in the victory scenes. Found in the vicinity of a temple believed to be dedicated to the storm god Baal on the basis of this stele, the relief showing the victorious weather god with his tree-weapon was probably set up to receive homage from the people of Ugarit. Thus, this scene fits within the category of the worship scene as discussed above; although worshippers are not depicted on the stele itself, they no doubt stood before it either within or before the temple.

On the Tell Mardikh/Ebla seal impression (Fig. 16) an enormous winged disc appears above the weather god and a human worshipper. The object in the outstretched hand of the storm god is unfortunately obliterated by damage to the impression but on the basis of the scenes discussed above, it may be that this scene, too, represents the victorious god after his conquest of the serpent.

Thus, these examples and the worship scenes we will discuss next make no clear reference to the battle. Rather, they allow the lightning, which represents fertility, to stand as the

---

[62] M.-Th. Barrelet, "Les déesses armées et ailées," *Syria* 32 (1955), 242-243.

[63] For example, see: Vanel, *L'Iconographie du dieu de l'orage*, 84. Also see C. Schaeffer, *Ugaritica II*, 121-130.

symbol of the storm god's victory over the serpent, which probably symbolizes forces of sterility and death.

A second type of worhip scene involved with the victory cycle shows not the weather god but the tree-weapon or vegetal standard surmounted by heavenly and solar emblems symbolic both of the god's victory and of the ultimate source of his tree-lightning as the object of homage and worship. This final scene in the narrative sequence portrays worship of the symbol of the fertility engendered by the god's victory over the snake and gives visual form to the eternal pact between the worshipper and the worshipped embodied by the tree standard. Numerous artifacts of Middle Bronze Age and later date show this ritual performed by 1) two kings, 2) a king and a suppliant goddess, 3) a single king, 4) composite figures like the griffin-demon and the bull-headed man. It is the first two types of scenes that will concern us here.[64]

Artifacts from Kültepe and Alalakh show two kingly figures worshipping the tree or standard or actually holding it with one outstretched hand. A seal impression from Kültepe *Karum* level Ib (Fig. 17) shows two kings flanking a volute standard with spear-like point. Surmounted by a crescent and disc, this volute standard is closely analogous to the volute and orb standards held by the weather god on impressions from Kültepe *Karum* level II (Figs. 4, 6). The stylized vegetal standards occur in the subsequent victory or worship scenes, but not in the actual battle scenes where the god holds a more realistically branching tree-weapon. The volute or vegetal standards surmounted by orbs or by wings seem to replace the victorious weather god approached by similar kings in contemporary worship scenes (Figs. 14, 15).

Several seal impressions from slightly later levels at Alalakh level VII show kings standing alongside vegetal standards surmounted by wings or orbs (Figs. 18, 19). The Alalakh seal impression shows two kings in identical caps and robes flanking a standard with curling volute summit supporting a crescent and orb (Fig. 18). Variations on these standards topped by curling vegetation appear in the form of similar tendrils embellishing the shafts or in an extremely artificial type of "trunk" composed of a series of round drillings.[65] A fragmentary Alalakh level VII seal impression (Fig. 19) shows the top of the latter type of standard branching into two pairs of tendrils surmounted by a round form and above this a winged disc.

Similar turned standards, presumably carved from wood and perhaps from the same tree used by the weather god in his battle, appear on numerous examples of Middle Bronze Age date flanked by two kings or by a king and a suppliant goddess.[66] Unlike the simple orb and crescent that surmount the simple volute standards with straight shafts (Figs, 17, 18), the turned standards are almost always surmounted by an elaborate winged disc, as on a seal in the Bibliothèque Nationale (Fig. 20).

Thus it appears that a complex cycle of images in Anatolian and Syrian art of the Middle Bronze Age (ca. 2000-1600 B.C.) centers upon the weather god's struggle with a serpent,

[64] For an example of a single king, see: L. Delaporte, *Catalogue des cylindres orientaux de la Bibliothèque Nationale*, (Paris, 1920), no. 491. For the griffin-demon, see: N. Özgüç, *Ancient Art in Seals*, ed. E. Porada, (Princeton, 1980), Fig. 6. For the bull-men, see: N. Özgüç, *Seals of Level Ib*, Pl. XXVI, 3.

[65] For example: E. Porada, *Corpus of Ancient Near Eastern Seals*, no. 955; Eisen, *Ancient Oriental Cylinders . . . Mrs. William H. Moore*, no. 12.

[66] For example: Williams-Forte, in *Ladders to Heaven*, ed. Oscar White Muscarella, (Toronto, 1981), no. 215.

his subsequent victory over it, his worship while holding the emblem of his victory, the tree-weapon or standard, and finally the worship or veneration of the victorious tree-standard.

Information concerning the nature of this foe of the weather god is provided by the visual imagery surrounding their battle. The snake appears to live beneath a mountain upon which the weather god stands when engaged in battle with that creature. The mountain appears to be the natural habitat of the god's tree, which he wields as a weapon in battle with the serpent. The association of the serpent with the earth beneath the mountain, namely the underworld, and the tree with living vegetation nourished by the fertilizing rains of the weather god suggests that the significance of this scene may lie in the realm of a battle between the forces of life represented by the weather god and his tree and the forces of death, symbolized by the serpent—the embodiment of all that is unformed and thus chaotic, according to Mircea Eliade.[67] The universal and cosmic nature of this struggle between life and death might then be suggested and perhaps explain the association of heavenly imagery with the victory scenes, when order, harmony, and stability have been restored following the battle of the weather god with the snake.

Identification of the serpent that appears in ancient Syrian pictorial representations of the first half of the second millennium B.C. with figures in texts have focused on the Ugaritic god of the sea, Yam, or one of his acolytes. The weather god Baal's struggle with a serpent on a seal in the Moore Collection in The Metropolitan Museum of Art has been interpreted by Pierre Amiet as representing that god's battle with the acolytes of Yam, the god of the sea, and his spouse Ashtarte, based on a myth known not from the Ugaritic cycle, but from Egyptian and later sources such as Philo of Byblos.[68] Vanel agrees with Amiet's interpretation that the snake represents Yam's monstrous acolyte.[69]

Until recently, references in the Ugaritic texts to a serpent or dragon have been considered as synonymous with the name Yam, (*ym*) sea, as well. This identification of the serpent with Yam is based partially on a passage in the Ugaritic Baal Epic in which Anat, the sister and perhaps consort of Baal, mentions Yam and other creatures that she has aided the storm god in conquering:

> What foe rises against Baal,
> what enemy against the rider on the clouds?
> Did I not destroy Yam the darling of El,
> did I not make an end of Nahar the great god?
> Was not the dragon captured and vanquished?
> I did destroy the wriggling serpent,
> the tyrant with seven heads;
> I did destroy Arsh the darling of the gods,
> I did silence Atik the calf of El,
> I did destroy Ishat the bitch of the gods,
> I did make an end of Zabib the daughter of El.

CTA 3.D.34-43 [70]

[67] As cited by N. J. Tromp, *Primitive Conceptions of Death and the Netherworld in the Old Testament*, Biblica et Orientalia, 21 (Rome, 1969) 164, n.29.

[68] Amiet, *Syria* 37 (1960), 8 and n.3.

[69] Vanel, *L'Iconographie du dieu de l'orage*, p. 93.

[70] J. C. L. Gibson, *Canaanite Myths and Legends* (Edinburgh, 1977), 50. In this article, I have made consistent the numbering of the Ugaritic texts on the basis of the system of A. Herdner, *Corpus des tablettes en cunéiformes alphabetiques découverts à Ras Shamra-Ugarit de 1919 à 1939* (Paris, 1963).

Although neither a serpent, *btn*, or dragon, *tnn*, are mentioned in connection with Yam in the Baal/Yam text, most scholars consider the dragon and serpent as identical to Yam-Nahar. This presumption appears based not upon firm evidence from the Ugaritic texts, but upon analogies with myths of other cultures, especially biblical passages that portray "Yahweh's battle with the monster." The equation of the serpent and the dragon with Yam in the Ugaritic texts depends on the appearance of the serpent in a later text (*CTA* 5.1.1) where it is called *ltn*, Lotan or Leviathan, but not Yam. On the basis of this text, which equates Lotan with the serpent, and the earlier Anat text quoted above which mentions Yam in sequence with the serpent and the dragon, however, many scholars have assumed all of these creatures to be manifestations of Yam, Prince Sea.[71]

Later biblical passages that mention a monster defeated by Yahweh are often cited as confirming the association of Yam with the dragon or serpent.[72] Even when not referring directly to the biblical passages, scholars presume an equation between serpents, dragons, and the sea not only in the Ugaritic texts but as well in the myths of other cultures. Kapelrud, in his study of the weather god, states "Lotan . . . was probably a common designation for a sea monster in the Ancient Near East."[73] He reasons that there are no texts telling about the struggle with Lotan/Tannin and thus this creature must be another sea monster mentioned in the texts, hence Yam.[74] Theodore Gaster uses the name of Yam interchangeably with the term "dragon." He states that "The first Tablet relates the triumph of Baal over the Dragon of the Sea (Yam)." Within a general category termed "The Defeat of the Dragon" (his "Comprehensive Type"), Gaster seems to equate all monsters of serpentine or dragonic form in the myths of other cultures as well as at Ugarit and to suggest that all these creatures are personifications of unruly waters or the sea.[75]

Other evidence suggests, however, that serpents and dragons are not necessarily sea monsters. In her recent study of "god's battle with the monster," Wakeman demonstrated that serpents and dragons appearing in Ancient Near Eastern, Indian and Greek myths are as often associated with mountains or fire as with water and may be "earth" monsters.[76] The Egyptian Apophis is the serpent on the mountain personifying the darkness that threatens the rise of the sun god Re each morning. The Greek Typhon is also associated with mountains and as well with flames. Described as having a hundred snake heads with flames darting from his eyes and roaring like a lion or bull, Typhon is also considered as a personification of the powers of dark earth. To capture him, Zeus burns off each of his heads and pins him under a mountain, Mt. Aetna.[77] Moreover, and most importantly, as other scholars have pointed out, Yam seems not to be identical to *tnn*, the dragon, or *btn*, the serpent. Miller states in his study of the divine warrior, "Yamm is not equated with these . . . figures . . . unless one assumes that because he appears in the list all the other creatures named are to

[71] Gaster, *Thespis*, 137-200; Kapelrud, *Ba'al*, 101-103; A. Jirku, *Der Mythus der Kanaaner* (Bonn, 1966), 28.

[72] This monster(s) in the Bible is called Yam, Rahab, Leviathan, or simply "dragon" (*tannin*) or "serpent" (*nāḥaš* or *bāšān*), see: Gibson, *Canaanite Myths*, 7. Also, see: F. M. Cross, *Canaanite Myth and Hebrew Epic: Essays in the History of Religion of Israel* (Cambridge, Mass., 1973), 120. Cassuto seems to consider the "dragon" as separate from the "serpent," see quote in footnote 1 above.

[73] A. Kapelrud, *Ba'al*, 101.

[74] *Ibid.*, 101-102 and 119.

[75] Gaster, *Thespis*, pp. 137-200, 28, 128 and 116.

[76] M. K. Wakeman, *God's Battle with the Monster* (Leiden, 1973), 15-43.

[77] *Ibid.*, 15-16, 31 and 9-12.

be identified with him."[78] Some commentators, most recently, Baruch Margalit, suggest that the serpent is the accomplice of Baal's other major adversary, Mot, or that this creature is Mot himself,[79] a possibility that we will turn to below.

The little information that is provided by the Baal/Yam text concerning the form taken by Yam suggests that his physical manifestation would reflect in some way his watery nature, based on his name and epithets which prove that he is the personification of the sea.[80] He is a god and presumably representations of his worship might exist.[81] According to several commentators, Yam may also be characterized by enormous size or "height."[82] Based on the pictorial representations discussed above, the serpent battled by the storm god, perhaps Baal, is neither associated with water, nor is it worshipped, nor is it enormous in size in comparison to the weather god.[83]

Perhaps most critical in the interpretation of the scenes showing the storm god battling a serpent and in the determination of the underlying nature and identity of this serpentine foe of the god is the representation of the weather god himself and his weapon. For the weapon wielded by the storm god against the serpent in the pictorial representations is the tree, seemingly symbolic of his lightning. Ugaritic texts, including passages from the Baal Epic, refer to the tree-lightning of Baal and to the "Cedar" that Baal brandishes against an adversary, probably Mot, following the opening of a window in his newly built palace (*CTA* 4.7.42). Critical for our discussion and for the interpretation of the identity of the serpent, however, is the fact that Baal gains his lightning only *after* his battle with and conquest of Yam, the god of the sea. Only with the building of Baal's palace on Mount Saphon, which symbolized the legitimacy of Baal's rule as king of the gods, following his defeat of Prince Yam, did his power to create the thunder and lightning take effect, as Clifford and others have shown.[84] As king, neither he nor his abilities were functional and legitimate until his enthronement within his palace. Thus, the tree-lightning could not have been used by Baal against his first foe, Yam, the sea,[85] suggesting that the serpent slain by

[78] P. Miller, *The Divine Warrior in Early Israel*, Harvard Semitic Monographs, 5 (Cambridge, Mass., 1973), 24.

[79] See: B. Margalit, *A Matter of "Life" and "Death": A Study of the Ba'al-Mot Epic (CTA 4-5-6)*, Altes Orient and Alter Testament, 206 (Neukirchen-Vluyn, 1980), 54, 63-67, 72-73, 83, 87-93, and 106. Also, see: U. Cassuto, "Baal and Mot in the Ugaritic Texts," *IEJ* 12 (1962), 77-86.

[80] See: O. Kaiser, *Die Mythische Bedeutung des Meeres in Ägypten, Ugarit, und Israel*, Zeitschrift fur die Alttestamentliche Wissenschaft, Beiheft 78 (Berlin, 1962), 44, 57-58, and 63; A. Caquot, M. Sznycer, and A. Herdner, *Textes Ougaritiques, I: Mythes et légendes* (Paris, 1974), 109-110.

[81] Yam appears in offering lists excavated at the site of Ras Shamra and in the Ugaritic pantheon text as the equivalent of the Babylonian deity *tamtu* or Tiamat, see: Dahood in *Le Antiche Divinità Semitiche*, Studi Semitici 1 (Rome, 1958), 91; J. Nougayrol, "Textes Religieux (18-19): 18. R. S. 20.24 ("Panthéon d'Ugarit")," in *Ugaritica V: Nouveaux texts accadiens, hourrites et ugaritiques des archives et bibliothèques privées d'Ugarit* (Paris, 1968), 45, line 29 and p. 58.

[82] See: Caquot, *et. al.*, *Textes Ougaritiques*, p. 136, n.k. and *CTA* 2.4.4-5, p. 135. Also, see: A. Van Selms, "Yammu's Dethronement by Ba'al: An Attempt to Reconstruct Texts UT 129, 137, and 68," *Ugarit Forschungen* 2 (1970), 265.

[83] For the suggestion by the present writer that the nude "hero" with streams may represent Yam, see: E. Williams-Forte in *Ladders to Heaven*, ed. Oscar White Muscarella, (Toronto, 1981), 245-246. For an alternate opinion, see, most recently: P. Amiet, "Jalons pour une interpretation du répertoire des sceaux-cylindres syriens au IIe millénaire," *Akkadica* 28 (1982), 19-40.

[84] See: Clifford, *The Cosmic Mountain*, esp. 69-72, 61-66, and 55-57.

[85] L. Fisher and F. B. Knutson, "An Enthronement Ritual at Ugarit," *JNES* 28 (1969), 157-167.

the storm god's tree-lightning in the art could not represent that deity, the first of Baal's foes.

The next enemy to challenge Baal in the Ugaritic cycle is the god of sterility, death, and the underworld: Mot. The first mention of Mot occurs in the text chronicling the building of Baal's palace symbolizing Baal's kingship which "mediates fertility and cosmic harmony."[86] Following a banquet celebrating Baal's victory over Yam and its culmination in the completion of his palace, Baal secures his kingdom by seizing cities in the surrounding countryside and then returns and places a window in his palace.

> Baal opened a window in the mansion
> a lattice in the midst of the palace
>   he opened a rift (in) the clouds
> Baal uttered his holy voice
> Baal repeated the issue of his lips

CTA 4.7.26-30[87]

The window in Baal's palace is literally "a rift in the clouds" through which he issues his "voice," thunder.[88] This cleft in the clouds, accompanied by thunder, presumably allows Baal's fertilizing rain to fall through to the earth; similar air holes in the firmament are credited as the source of rain in later biblical texts.[89] In the following lines (CTA 4.7.31-41), Baal's "voice" is said to make the earth and mountains quake and his "tree" (arz) to strike fear into the heart of his enemy.[90] This adversary is probably Mot or his helpers, who seem to either invade Baal's territory or occupy the forests and inhabit the interior of the mountain.[91] Although the "tree" that Baal brandishes in his right hand is generally agreed to represent his lightning,[92] the type of tree meant by arz is variously rendered as "yew," "fir," or "cedar."[93] Support for the relationship of trees to the lightning of Baal is provided by a new text from Ugarit (RS 24.245) which may also belong to the events of CTA 3.3 leading up to the building of Baal's palace.[94] As interpreted by Fisher and Knutson, Baal's thunder and lightning are juxtaposed in this text to the statement, "The tree

---

[86] Clifford, *The Cosmic Mountain*, 69.

[87] Gibson, *Canaanite Myths*, 65.

[88] For thunder, see: Caquot, *et. al.*, *Textes Ougaritiques*, 217, II AB Vii, line 28 and n. h. Also, see: Fisher and Knutson, *JNES* 28 (1969), 159, n.11.

[89] J. De Moor, *The Seasonal Pattern in the Ugaritic Myth of Ba'lu According to the Version of Ilimiku*, Alter Orient und Altes Testament, 16 (Neukirchen-Vluyn, 1971), 162-163; Caquot, *et. al.*, *Textes Ougaritiques*, 188; Gaster, *Thespis*, 175.

[90] De Moor, *The Seasonal Pattern in the Ugaritic Myth of Ba'lu*, 164, line 41 and Pl. 67; Caquot, *et. al*, *Textes Ougaritiques*, 211, n. g., 216-218, I AB vii, lines 35-42; Gibson, *Canaanites Myths*, 65 CTA IV. VII, line 41. For a different opinion on this passage, see: B. Margalit, *A Matter of "Life" and "Death,"* 63-65.

[91] U. Cassuto, "The Palace of Baal," *Journal of Biblical Literature* 61 (1942), 56; De Moor, *The Seasonal Pattern in the Ugaritic Myth of Ba'lu*, 47.

[92] Caquot, *et. al.*, *Textes Ougaritiques*, 217 II AB vii, lines 35-36.

[93] For fir, see: De Moor, *The Seasonal Pattern in the Ugaritic Myth of Ba'lu*, 167. For cedar, see: Caquot, *et. al.*, *Textes Ougaritiques*, 218, n.p. For, yew, see: "Ugaritic Myths, Epics and Legends," *Ancient Near Eastern Texts*, ed. J. B. Pritchard (Philadelphia, 1955), 135, line 41. And also, see: Fisher and Knutson, *JNES* 28 (1969), 159, n.11.

[94] Fisher and Knutson, *JNES* 28 (1969), 161-167 and M. Pope and J. Tigay, "A Description of Ba'al," *Ugarit Forschungen*, 3 (1971), 117-130.

of lightning he (Baal) creates."[95] They call attention as well to the Papyrus Leyden 345, an Egyptian document of New Kingdom date which states "Baal smites thee with the cedar tree which is in his hand."[96] Thus, the tree or lightning recently gained by Baal following his enthronement is his weapon in the battle with Mot on the basis of *CTA* 4.7.35-49. Following the opening of the window and the issuing of his holy voice, Baal brandshes his lightning in tree form as a weapon against his foe on earth, namely Mot.

The action which symbolizes the fruition of his powers as king and as the mediator of fertility, the opening of a window in his newly built palace, ironically also creates a "breach" that permits his adversaries once again to threaten his domain and kingship, setting the stage for his confrontation with his second and most persistent challenger, Mot. An epic combat begins between Baal, god of fertility, and thus of life, and Mot, or death, following the completion of Baal's palace and reoccurs "seven years" later. In the initial conflict Baal and the order he symbolizes succumb to Mot and the forces of chaos. Baal descends to Mot's netherworld abode and rain disappears from the earth. In the end, however, Baal triumphs over Mot and fertility and cosmic order are restored.[97]

In the pictorial representations, the tree-lightning used to slay the serpent appears in the shape of a conifer having an erect stem and horizontal branches covered in fern-like needles rather than flat leaves[98] (Figs. 8, 9, 10). Such conifers, found predominantly in the highlands of temperate regions such as the mountains of the Levant, renowned for cedars,[99] recall the tree, the Ugaritic word, *arz*, most frequently translated cedar, that serves as Baal's lightning and which he brandishes against the god Mot.

What can be discerned, therefore, from the Ugaritic texts concerning the nature and possible form taken by the god Mot? In contrast to Baal's first opponent, the god of the sea Yam, there has been surprisingly little conjecture concerning the shape taken by Mot. Claude Schaeffer proposes that Mot takes human form. He suggested that a damaged stele from Ras Shamra/Ugarit showing a warrior holding a *was* scepter and resembling Egyptian representations of Seth depicted Mot, a deity who, like Seth, killed his brother, namely Baal.[100] Schaeffer's identification of this stele as Mot, however, was at least partially based on the assumption that a deity of Mot's importance would have been represented on at least one of the stelae excavated at Ras Shamra/Ugarit.[101] Recent texts from Ugarit prove, however, that Mot—perhaps due to his negative role in the mythological cycle—was not listed in the pantheon or offering lists.[102] It seems unlikely, therefore, that the figure on this stele, which was set up in the temple area as the probable focus of worship or offerings, represents the rapacious netherworld deity Mot.

[95] See: Fisher and Knutson, *JNES* 28 (1969), 159, lines 3-4.

[96] *Ibid.*, 159. Also, see: J. Wilson, "The Egyptians and the Gods of Asia," *Ancient Near Eastern Texts*, ed. J. Pritchard, (Princeton, 1955), 249.

[97] See: B. Margalit, *A Matter of "Life" and "Death"* and P. L. Watson, "Mot, the God of Death at Ugarit and in the Old Testament" Diss. Yale University 1970.

[98] See, for example: W. Harris, and J. Levy, "Conifer," in *The New Columbia Encyclopedia* (London and New York, 1975), 2153.

[99] See: C. Gadd, "The Dynasty of Agade and the Gutian Invasion," *Cambridge Ancient History* I/1, 425-426 and A. Malamat, "Campaigns to the Mediterranean by Iaḥdunlim and Other Early Mesopotamian Rulers," *Assyriological Studies 16: Studies in Honor of Benno Landsberger* (Chicago, 1965), p. 1, n.1.

[100] C. Schaeffer, *Ugaritica II*, 93-95, 99-104, Pl. XXII, 3.

[101] *Ibid.*, 102.

[102] See above note 81.

Haran and Løkkegaard look to the sarcophagus of Ahiram as a likely place for iconography related to the god of death in the Syro-Palestinian region.[103] Haran identified the enthroned male figure on the basis of the inscription reading the "staff of judgment," which he identified as the figure's wilted lotus, rejecting earlier interpretations of his emblem as Ahiram's "staff of sovereignty." Løkkegaard, too, refers to the sarcophagus of Ahiram for information concerning the shape of "death," but finds the lions supporting the tomb "as representatives of the netherworld" rather than the human figures above. He states that "if it is possible to identify Mot with any animal it must be a roaring lion,"[104] but provides no supportive evidence.

In turning to the Ugaritic texts *CTA* 4-6 for information concerning this god, it is clear that Mot is characterized as living in the underworld, as having an enormous devouring mouth and appetite, and as supervising aridity and sterility.[105] Mot's name is generally agreed to derive from the word *mt*, "to die," and thus means death. Like Yam, Baal's first antagonist, Mot is the son of El (*bn · ilm · mt*)[106] and presumably also of El's consort, Asherah, and is called "El's beloved" (*mdd · ilm · mt*) and additionally "the hero, beloved of El" (*ydd · il · ġzr*).[107] Unlike Yam, however, Mot does not seem to have been worshipped as a god at Ugarit, as discussed above. Mot dwells in the underworld, leaving no doubt that he is the embodiment of death.[108] Entrance to Mot's underworld abode lies beneath two mountains that mark the frontier of the inhabited world and the entrance to the land of the dead.[109] Another more horrifying mode of entrance into the netherworld is by way of Mot's "gullet," for his rapacious nature is represented in an open mouth that threatens to devour all living things.[110]

Mot's connection with sterility and drought is two-fold, for not only is his underworld abode sometimes described as arid steppe, like the Sheol of the Old Testament as Clifford has pointed out,[111] but with the disappearance down Mot's gullet of Baal, the god of rain and thus fertility, the earth above becomes sterile and dry. Mot thus causes drought and death on the earth, and according to Watson, controls Shapash, the sun goddess, who reigns in the heavens during Baal's absence.[112]

Mot's devouring mouth, abode in the netherworld beneath two mountains, and association with sterility and death . . . also characterize the serpent in the pictorial representations, perhaps providing the most critical evidence for the corelation of the snake with Mot. The snake battled by the storm god frequently rises up from beneath the mountains upon which the god stands (Fig. 10). The serpent's tail remains hidden underground in the battle and victory scenes, providing visual evidence that its original abode actually lies beneath the earth and the mountains, thus in the netherworld (Figs. 1, 2). The city of Mot, in the

[103] M. Haran, "The Bas-reliefs on the Sarcophagus of Ahiram, King of Byblos," *IEJ* 8 (1957), 15-25.

[104] Føkkegaard, "A Plea for El, the Bull, and Other Ugaritic Miscellanies," in *Studia Orientalia Joanni Pedersen septuagenario dictata* (Copenhagen, 1953), 231.

[105] Watson, "Mot, The God of Death," 136-147.

[106] J. Gray, *The Legacy of Canaan*, Supplements to *Vetus Textamentum*, 5 (Leiden, 1957), 47; A. Cassuto, *The Goddess Anath*, (Jerusalem, 1971), 55.

[107] Watson, "Mot, The God of Death," 136-138.

[108] Caquot, *et. al.*, *Textes Ougaritiques*, 231.

[109] *Ibid.*, 230-231.

[110] *Ibid.*, 219, n.2. Also, see: Gibson, *Canaanite Myths*, 16.

[111] Clifford, *The Cosmic Mountain*, 81-85.

[112] Watson, "Mot, The God of Death," 146. Also, see: Gibson, *Canaanite Myths*, 53, n.8.

texts, is said to lie beneath two mountains and perhaps it is from beneath these two mountains marking the entrance to the land of the dead that the serpent, perhaps Mot, rises against the storm god, perhaps Baal, in these representations. The open devouring mouth of Mot, a constant motif in the Ugaritic texts, symbolizing the god's rapacious nature threatening to devour all living things, seems also to find visual form in the portrayal of the serpent. In the battle scenes, the snake's mouth is portrayed gaping open with the god's tree-lightning thrust into it. For the snake to have swallowed the god's weapon, its mouth must have been open, baring its perhaps poisonous fangs and threatening the storm god with its bite (Figs. 8, 9, 10). Indeed, in the texts, prior to the fertility god Baal's victory over Mot, he himself is "devoured" by the god of death, descending into the netherworld through Mot's open mouth and with his descent rain and fertility disappear from the earth. Thus the monstrous serpent capable of propelling itself from its underworld abode in the pictorial representations of the second millennium B.C. in Syria may represent Mot, the embodiment of death. The identification of the serpent and the weather god's weapon in the identical Anatolian material is problematic but seems clearly to embody a similar concept of the battle between forces of life/fertility and death/sterility.[113]

It is perhaps relevant that the Old Testament as well as other Christian and Hebrew texts provide as many, if not more, cases of serpents' association with death and the netherworld as with the "unruly waters" conquered by Yahweh. In his study of "primitive" conceptions of death and the netherworld in the Old Testament, Tromp points out that the serpent is frequently associated with death and that in the later books of the Bible, Satan is identified with a serpent. In Christian Coptic literature, as well, the serpent is portrayed as the devil that approaches Judas, who prays: "Lord, he came to me in the shape of a snake, while his mouth opened and he wanted to devour me."[114] The image of Satan and of the entrance to Hell as rapacious and devouring is nowhere better illustrated than in the "Hell's mouths" in scenes of the Last Judgment and the Harrowing of Hell in medieval architectural sculpture and book illustration (Pl. II-4).

In Genesis III, the serpent is generally considered as a symbol of evil and of cunning but not of death for it is in later Biblical texts that the serpent is most clearly equated with death and the devil. However, as F. Hvidberg has pointed out in his discussion of Genesis III, the serpent was not a giver of life but on the contrary he brought death instead of life: he was the deceiver. The serpent, according to Hvidberg, is synonymous not with Satan but with an earlier great adversary of Yahweh for the soul of Israel, Baal.[115] The connection of storm god, tree and serpent in the early pictorial, and possibly textual traditions of the "Lands of the Bible" may provide the link, previously missing, between these figures that will allow further inquiry into the precise significance of the evil snake's appearance in the tree in the garden.

---

[113] Both Hittite and Hurrian myths relate the storm god's battles with creatures perhaps symbolic of forces of infertility. See the Illuyankas myth: A. Goetze, "Hittite Myths, Epics and Legends," in *Ancient Near Eastern Texts*, ed., J. Pritchard (Princeton, 1969), 125-126. See the Hedammu myth: H. G. Güterbock, *Kumarbi, Mythen von Churritischen Kronos*, Istanbuler Schriften 16 (Zurich, 1946), 116 ff. For a discussion of the late Hittite Empire relief from Malatya showing the weather god's battle with a serpent and problems concerning that creatures identification as the dragon Illuyankas, see: H. G. Güterbock, "Narration in Anatolian, Syrian, and Assyrian Art," *American Journal of Archaeology*, 60 (1955), 64 and n.15.

[114] Tromp, *Primitive Conceptions of Death*, 164-166.

[115] F. Hvidberg, *Vetus Testamentum*, 10/3 (1960), 288-289.

In conclusion, the choice of a specific type of tree, a conifer, in the early "Canaanite" visual and textual material that we have been discussing, as the tree-symbol of the weather god's lightning and as the weapon he wields against the serpent, perhaps the god of death, Mot, seems particularly appropriate. Conifers, such as the cedar, are evergreen trees that maintain their foliage throughout the changing seasons. The storm god thus slays the serpent of death with virtually a "tree of life." When it is recalled that the "cedar" weapon symbolizes, as well, the lightning source of the weather god's fertility with which he then slays the embodiment of the drought, perhaps Mot, the serpent, this representation is revealed as a complex visual image embodying several levels of symbolic meaning, much in the manner of the complicated metaphorical language of the texts.

Figure 1
Detail of an Old Anatolian style seal impression from Kültepe *Karum* level II. After, N. Özgüç, *The Anatolian Group of Cylinder Seal Impressions from Kültepe*, Türk Tarih Kurumu Yayınlarından, 5 serie, 22 (Ankara, 1965) pl. XXIV, 71.

Figure 2
Drawing of a cylinder seal impression of an Old Anatolian style seal on a tablet in the British Museum by D. Collon. After, P. Garelli and D. Collon, *Cuneiform Texts from Cappadocian Tablets in the British Museum*, Part VI (London, 1975), no. 14.

Figure 3
Drawing of a detail of an Old Anatolian style seal impression from Kültepe *Karum* level II. After, N. Özgüç, *The Anatolian Group*, pl. X, 29.

Figure 4
Drawing of a detail of an Old Syrian cylinder seal impression from Kültepe *Karum* level II. After, T. and N. Özgüç, *Kültepe Kazisi Raporu 1949*, Türk Tarih Kurumu Yayınlarından, V serie, 12 (Ankara, 1953), no. 692.

Figure 5

Drawing of a detail of an Old Syrian style seal impression from Kültepe *Karum* level II. After, T. and N. Özgüç, *Kültepe 1949, no. 691.*

Figure 6

Drawing of a detail of an Old Syrian style seal impression from Kültepe level Ib. After, N. Özgüç, *Seals and Seal Impressions of Level Ib from Karum Kanesh*, Türk Tarih Kurumu Yayınlarından, 5 serie, 25 (Ankara, 1968), pl. XXII, 2.

Figure 7

Drawing of a detail of a Syrian seal from a Roman tomb; now in Florence. After, H. T. Bossert, *Altsyrien*, (Tubingen, 1951), no. 852.

Figure 8

Drawing of an impression of a Syrian cylinder seal in the British Museum, BM 89514. With the kind permission of E. Porada.

Figure 9

Drawing of a detail of an impression of a Syrian cylinder seal, Louvre A918 by David Castriota. Published by L. Delaporte, *Catalogue des cylindres, cachets et pierre gravées de style oriental, Volume I.* Musée du Louvre, (Paris, 1920).

Figure 10

Drawing of a detail of an impression of a Syrian cylinder seal in the Seyrig Collection in the Bibliothèque Nationale in Paris. Seyrig Collection 108. With the kind permission of R. Curiel.

Figure 11

Drawing of an impression of a Syrian cylinder seal in the collection of the Pierpont Morgan Library. Published by E. Porada, *Corpus of Ancient Near Eastern Seals in North American Collections*, (Washington, D.C., 1948), no. 967. After H. el-Safadı, "Die Entstehung der syrischen Glyptik und ihre Entwicklung in der Zeit von Zimrilim bis Ammitaqumma," Inaugural-Dissertation, Berlin, 1968, Abb. 64.

Figure 12

Drawing of a detail of an impression of a Syrian cylinder seal in the Staatlichen Münzsammlung in München. Published by U. Moortgat-Correns, "Altorientalische Rollsiegel in der Staatlichen Münzsammlung in München," *Münchner Jahrbuch der bildenden Kunst*, 6 (1955) pl. III, 24. After, H. el-Safadi, "Die Enstehung der syrischen Glyptik . . . " Abb. 126.

Figure 13

Drawing of a detail of an impression of a Syrian cylinder seal in the Yale Babylonian Collection (YBC 1222) by David Castriota. Published by B. Buchanan, *Early Near Eastern Seals in the Yale Babylonian Collection*, ed. Ulla Kasten (New Haven and London, 1981) YBC 1222.

Figure 14

Drawing of a detail of an impression of a Syrian cylinder in the collection of the Musée du Louvre, Paris. Louvre AO 10871. With the kind permission of P. Amiet.

Figure 15

Drawing of the "Baal au foudre" stele from Ras Shamra/Ugarit. Musée du Louvre. After A. Caquot, "La Religion à Ugarit," in *Le Monde de la Bible*, ed. P. Bockel, (Paris, n.d.) pl. 25.

Figure 16

Drawing of a detail of a seal impression of Syrian style on a vessel from Tell Mardikh/Ebla. After P. Matthiae, "Empreintes d'un cylindre paléosyrien de Tell Mardikh." *Syria* 46 (1969), 1-43.

Figure 17

Drawing of a detail of an impression of a Syrian style seal from Kültepe *Karum* level Ib. After N. Özgüç, *Seals of Level Ib*, pl. XXIX, 2.

Figure 18

Drawing of a detail of a seal impression of Syrian style from Tell Atchana/Alalakh level VII, by Dominique Collon. After D. Collon, *The Seal Impressions from Tell Atchana/Alalakh*, Alter Orient und Altes Testament, 27 (Neukirchen-Vluyn, 1975), no. 76.

Figure 19

Drawing of a seal impression of Syrian style from Tell Atchana/Alalakh level VII. After D. Collon, *The Seal Impressions from Alalakh*, no. 53.

Figure 20

Drawing of a detail of an impression of a Syrian cylinder seal in the Bibliothèque Nationale in Paris. Published by L. Delaporte, *Catalogue des cylindres orientaux de la Bibliothèque Nationale*. (Paris, 1920), no. 435. After H. el-Safadi, "Die Entstehung der syrischen Glyptik . . . " Abb. 107.

SEAL MANUFACTURE IN THE LANDS OF THE BIBLE: RECENT FINDINGS *

A. JOHN GWINNETT

S.U.N.Y. at Stony Brook, New York

LEONARD GORELICK

S.U.N.Y. at Stony Brook, New York

While there are about sixty references to seals in the Old and New Testaments, none give even a clue as to how they were made. The references are either metaphoric, e.g. "...he received the sign of circumcision, a seal of the righteousness of the faith..." [Romans 15.28], or allude to their bureaucratic function, e.g., "So she [Jezebel] wrote letters in Ahab's name and sealed them with his seal and sent the letters unto the elders" [Kings 21.8].

The absence of textual material is not surprising. Indeed, it is consistent with the fact that there is no ancient writing in all of the Near East on this subject. Consequently, information on methods used to manufacture seals has been derived in other ways. Our approach has been experimental.

The purpose of this paper is to describe our recent research on one particular aspect of seal production, namely, how they were drilled.

There were four original findings that are of special interest. The first provided an excellent clue as to the type of drill used on particular micro-crystalline quartz seals. The second resolved an important scholarly controversy in the history of ancient lapidary and yielded a clue as to how to determine the type of abrasive used in drilling. The third supplied evidence for a type of drill that anticipated the contemporary bonded abrasive drill by almost five thousand years. The fourth verified a previous finding concerning a specific type of drill employed on an agate stamp seal of the Achaemenid period.

Some of the procedures involved in this investigation have been previously reported. They have been used to analyze: beads from Shahr-i-Sokhta,[1] an Early Bronze Age site in eastern Iran; ancient Near Eastern cylinder seals;[2,3] the drilled, inlaid teeth of the ancient

*The authors would like to express their gratitude to Drs. Bernard Botthmer, Robert Bianchi, Richard Fazzini and James Romano of the Brooklyn Museum and Dr. Robert Brill of the Corning Glass Museum for their cooperation and assistance in this project.

[1] A. John Gwinnett and Leonard Gorelick, "Beadmaking in Iran in the Early Bronze Age," *Expedition* 1981, 10-23.

[2] A. John Gwinnett and Leonard Gorelick, "Ancient Lapidary: A Study Using Scanning Electron Microscopy and Functional Analysis," *Expedition* 1979, 17-32.

[3] Leonard Gorelick and A. John Gwinnett, "The Origin and Development of the Ancient Near Eastern Cylinder Seal," *Expedition* 1981, 17-30.

Maya;[4] an Early Bronze Age Cycladic statuette;[5] stone statuettes exhibited at the Cleveland Musem;[6] and a drilled Old Kingdom sarcophagus lid in the Brooklyn Museum.[7]

There are three separate steps in our method of study, all non-destructive to the object. They are: 1) silicone impressions of the parts to be studied in order to capture the tool marks; 2) examination of the tool marks on the impressions in the scanning electron microscope (SEM); and 3) functional analysis in order to duplicate the tool marks experimentally. We have made the analogy with this type of functional analysis to ballistics, where one can identify the bullet from the bullet hole. In this inquiry, the objective was to obtain insight into the unknown, missing drills and the abrasives from the extant drill marks. We made over fifty drill holes experimentally using various abrasives and drills which will be described later in the text.

1. Evidence for the Use of a Copper Drill

In a previously published study of twenty-nine micro-crystalline quartz cylinder seals, ranging from the Early Dynastic period ca. 2500 B.C. to the Neo-Assyrian period ca. 800 B.C., a puzzling, peculiar shape was observed on the silicone impressions of ten of the drill holes. These shapes, positive on the impressions, and therefore negative in the drill holes, were named "collars" (Pl. III-1a). The finding of these "collars" was a surprise and no reason for their occurrence was evident at that time. Proof was forthcoming, however, in the present study when the "collar" shape was unexpectedly produced during the course of experimental drilling using a copper rod on glass with a loose abrasive (Pl. III-1b). As drilling continued, a second collar shape appeared in a manner similar to that seen on several of the cylinder seals previously described. None were produced to date using flint or wooden drills. It is our guess that collars occur, at times, as part of the sequence of tool wear when copper is used to drill hard stones for a lengthy period.

Since collars were found on seals made before the use of iron tools, it strongly suggests that drills used in the group of the ten seals previously reported were made of copper or bronze. There are two potential uses for this finding: first, if collars cannot be formed using an iron drill, then their presence in a drill hole may serve as a means of dating seals that cannot be dated stylistically; and, second, as a means of authenticating dubious seals of unknown provenance that contain collars.

2. A Scholarly Controversy Partly Resolved

Nearly all the impressions we have taken from drill holes of cylinder seals have shown regular concentric lines throughout. These are similar to the ones observed by Sir Flinders Petrie[8] on granite cores made by tubular drills during the Old Kingdom period in Egypt.

[4] A. John Gwinnett and Leonard Gorelick, "Inlayed Teeth of Ancient Mayans: A Tribologic Study Using the SEM," *SEM Inc.*, 1979 Vol. 1, 575-580.

[5] A. John Gwinnett and Leonard Gorelick, "An Ancient Repair on a Cycladic Statuette Analyzed Using Scanning Electron Microsopy," *Journal of Field Archeology*. In press.

[6] A. John Gwinnett and Leonard Gorelick, "An Innovative Method for Authenticating Drilled Stone Artifacts of Unknown Provenance," *MASCA*. In press.

[7] Leonard Gorelick and A. John Gwinnett, "Did the Ancient Egyptians Use Fixed Points for Drilling?" *Expedition*. Submitted for publication.

[8] W. M. Flinders Petrie, *Tools and Weapons*, Warminster, England, 1917, 44 and 45.

Petrie stated that "only fixed cutting points" could have created such regular concentric tracks. Lucas,[9] an equal authority on ancient Egyptian technology, disagreed, stating that the Egyptians did not possess the necessary technology to make "fixed points." He felt certain that only a loose abrasive was used, conceding only that the loose abrasive of wet sand might have become embedded or charged to the copper drill during usage. Petrie suggested that emery was the abrasive that was used. Neither offered proof for their conclusions.

As a result of our experimental drilling, we are fairly certain that the regular concentric lines of the type observed on drilled granite cores by both Lucas and Petrie can provide an important clue as to both the type of abrasive and the method used. It also allows for a partial resolution of their controversy over the utilization of fixed cutting points.

Our evidence, based on the following experimental procedures, falls into the general category of "functional analysis."

1) A slab of granite was drilled with a copper rod and/or a copper tube in conjunction with the following abrasives; (their Mohs scale of hardness is placed alongside in parenthesis) a] beach sand (7), b] crushed quartz (7), c] garnet (7), d] emery (9), e] corundum (9), f] silicon carbide (9.5), g] diamond (10). Granite is an intrusive igneous rock containing quartz (7), feldspar (6) and mica (2-3).

2) Drilling was also attempted with a] chipped flint, b] shaped sandstone, and c] shaped quartzite.

3) These abrasives were used either a] dry, b] wet, c] in a grease-like vehicle or lubricant, d] olive oil, e] experimentally glued (by us) to a copper rod, or f] on a contemporary bonded drill.

4) The size of the abrasives varied to include 60-90 grit and 240 grit.

5) Drilling was effected at a constant rotational speed of 1000 RPM and held intermittently at a relatively constant pressure.

6) Some drilling was done with an oscillating brace bit in a back and forth manner and some with a bow drill.

FINDINGS. The clue that provided the basis for partly resolving the difference of opinion between Lucas and Petrie resulted from the experimental procedures described above. This happened when it became evident that it was possible to drill granite without creating concentric abrasion lines. Therefore, an abrasive that could effect drilling but did not produce cutting lines in the stone would be ruled out as a possibility. This occurred when sand and crushed quartz were used with either a copper rod or copper tube. No lines occurred when these were added loose, either dry or wet (Pl. IV-2a). Therefore, Lucas was wrong that wet sand was the abrasive used since the surface was totally rough. An examination of the drills after drilling with sand or quartz failed to reveal any charging of these to the copper. With this result Lucas' second hypothesis—that attachment occurred during drilling—was disproved.

On the other hand, Petrie was right in one respect and possibly wrong in another. He was correct in that emery could have been used since we found its use with a copper tube produced concentric cutting lines (Pl. IV-b). He was wrong in that it did *not require* that

[9] A. Lucas, *Ancient Egyptian Materials and Techniques*, 1962 4th ed.

it be used as fixed points to create the cutting lines. While we were able to glue emery to a copper rod and while lines were produced in granite at the leading edge of drilling, drilling did not advance enough to produce concentric lines on side walls. There are many reasons for this, such as loss of the cutting edge of the fixed particles, wear of the glue, etc. Our gluing was done using a combination of hide glue and water glass (sodium silicate), both of which were within the technology of the ancient Egyptians. It is possible that there are methods of creating fixed points that we have not tried as yet, such as embedding abrasives in a melt of copper to produce the equivalent of a contemporary sintered drill. Future work may help to clarify this issue.

Emery did not produce concentric lines when it was used dry. It produced lines when used in a water slurry which helped to keep the abrasive at the drill site and on track, so to speak. This would suggest that the ancient Egyptians were aware of the value of water as an aid to drilling—something that contemporary lapidaries still employ.

Emery also produced lines when used in conjunction with a viscous lubricant and with olive oil. These, too, served to keep the abrasive particles at the site of drilling. It is not possible to say for certain which method was employed. Utilizing a viscous lubricant also had the advantage of being able to create a drill hole faster than when water was mixed with the abrasive. Further research is needed to distinguish between the use of different vehicles for the abrasives.

Concentric cutting lines were present after drilling with corundum and diamond (Pls. V-3a, V-3b). These occurred when the abrasives were used loose with water, olive oil or a viscous lubricant. Only diamond produced concentric lines when used loose and dry. More experimentation is required to differentiate between drilling created by emery, corundum and diamond, and also between drilling with water or a lubricant as an adjunct.

Experimental drilling with chipped flint, fashioned sandstone and quartzite produced neither concentric lines nor a drill hole on granite, thereby precluding their use. It is tempting to believe that emery was the abrasive used because of the well-known statement by Pliny that emery or naxium was available from Naxos. This may have been the Egyptian source for the abrasive. Turkey also produces emery but there is no proof that this was known and/or utilized in ancient times.

Due to its tremendous efficiency, it is also intriguing to speculate that diamond was the abrasive. One reason for this efficiency can be seen in the graph by Woodall (Pl. VI-4) which shows that while emery and corundum are 9.5 on the Mohs scale and diamond is 10, there is a significant fourfold increment between them. Petrie also speculated on the use of diamond and then rejected it because of its "rarity."

At this stage in our research, we cannot say for sure which one of the abrasives that created concentric cutting lines in the granite, i.e. emery, corundum and diamond, was the one that was used or, indeed, if all were known or employed.

These findings raise a number of significant questions. If the abrasive was not emery but corundum or diamond, from whence did it come, since neither are thought to be indigenous to Egypt? Were they and the method of using water or a lubricant known to the lapidaries of the surrounding regions? Were they used on the other hard stones? When was their use first discovered? Can the presence or absence of concentric lines be used as indicators of the abrasive used on other stones? Can these lines provide a method to distinguish genuine from forged artifacts? Answers to these questions will, hopefully, result from future study.

3. Creating Bonded Abrasives

Experiments were conducted in order to determine if abrasives could be attached to a copper rod using various glues possibly known in ancient times. These glues included bitumen, pitch, tar, asphalt, casein, hide glue and water glass. Successful gluing and subsequent drilling with the production of concentric lines was achieved using hide glue on a copper rod (Pl. VI-5). This occurred in experimental drilling on glass but not on granite. The hide glue-water glass combination used in the experiment is still being made commercially and employed by lapidaries as a polishing aid. According to Robert Brill,[10] Research Scientist at the Corning Museum of Glass, the manufacture of water glass was well within the technology of the ancient world in which the production of glass and glazes had been accomplished. The difference between water glass and typical ancient glass is that the latter is made with about 65% sand and some soda ash, whereas water glass required 1-4% sand and large amounts of soda ash. The increase in soda ash, according to Dr. Brill, lowers the melting point of the batch and is, therefore, easier to produce than ordinary glass.

Although gluing was effective in producing a bonded abrasive, which produced concentric lines during drilling on glass, it is not possible to be certain that this was the actual method used. In theory, other, equally or more effective means are conceivable.

4. Evidence for a Tubular Drill

In a previous study, an impression was made of the drill hole of an agate stamp seal from the Achaemenid period (Pls. VII-6a, VII-6b). This seal was of particular interest because the craftsman had made an error and discontinued drilling after proceeding part of the way. The result was a dead end. Consequently, the silicone impression captured the result of the leading edge of the drill. When examined in the SEM, it seemed evident that there was a conchoidal fracture pattern. We deduced that this occurred when a core created by a tubular drill was broken off. In the present study, this observation was shown by experimental duplication. Using a tubular drill on an agate slab, a core was formed and broken off. Figures 71a-d show scanning micrographs of the drill hole. There are specific characteristics produced by the leading edge of a tubular copper drill, even when a core is not present, that clearly distinguishes it from the leading edge of a solid copper drill. The end is rounded, distinctly polished with some fine concentric lines; a solid copper drill produces rounding without polishing, roughness without lines and in certain stages, deep grooves.

In summary, then, evidence has been presented:

1) To explain the presence of peculiar collar shapes which, in turn, may be indicators of the use of a copper drill.

2) To partly resolve an important scholarly controversy that "fixed cutting points" for drilling were technically feasible in the ancient world. In turn, this has important implications in the history of ancient lapidary and has not been previously proven. The presence of concentric lines found on drill holes provides a clue as to the abrasive and to the method that was used, which may have included a viscous lubricant such as olive oil or grease. Our new findings show: a] loose, dry abrasives *did not* produce concentric lines (except diamond), b] fixed abrasives or those in a watery slurry or a lubricant such as olive oil *did*

[10] Robert Brill. Personal communication.

produce concentric cutting lines, 3] corundum and diamond cannot be ruled out as not having been used to drill granite.

3) To demonstrate that "fixed cutting points" for drilling could have been made by gluing, using materials available at the time.

4) To verify an observation about the use of a tubular drill in an agate stamp seal of the Achaemenid period.

These four findings reinforce our view that our method of investigation has practical value in discovering and understanding ancient lapidary procedures.

HEBREW SEALS OF OFFICIALS

RUTH HESTRIN

Israel Museum, Jerusalem, Israel

This short review of Hebrew seals belonging to officials relates to the last two centuries of the Monarchy, that is, from the 8th to the early 6th century B.C.E. Most of the known inscribed Hebrew seals belong to that period, including both decorated seals and seals bearing only inscriptions. The decorated seals are more common in the 8th century, while those bearing solely inscriptions predominate in the 7th and 6th centuries.

The main function of the seals, which came into widespread use in the first half of the first millennium, was to serve as a mark of ownership. Another source of information concerning seals comes from bullae—bits of wet clay impressed with a seal, which served to seal rolled-up papyrus documents. This explains the expression "a sealed book" in Isaiah 29:11. Archaeological evidence shows that pottery vessels containing oil, wine, or other valuable products were closed with clay stoppers, which were then impressed with a seal. Written testimony to this practice can be found in some Hebrew ostraca from Arad,[1] which contain orders to royal functionaries to seal with their seals the jars containing oil which had been issued at the citadel.

Most of the seals bear the name of their owner, preceded by the possessive *lamed* and followed by the word *ben* and the patronymic. An especially important group is that of seals inscribed with the names and titles of ministers or other royal functionaries. The Bible mentions many functionaries in the royal administration, but their specific functions are often difficult to determine. Of these offices, the following are also found on seals:

ROYAL STEWARD, אשר על הבית "who is over the (royal) house." This was the most important official. The Bible mentions holders of this title during the reigns of Elah, Ahab, and Jehu of Israel, and during the reign of Hezekiah of Judah. The title is mentioned on a bulla from Lachish[2] and in a tomb-inscription[3] from Jerusalem of the late 8th century B.C.E.

SCRIBE, סופר . In Israel, as in the other countries of the ancient Near East, the scribes were among the highest officials at the royal court and their office was hereditary in certain families. The status of the royal scribe was particularly high, and his office was located within the king's house. The family of Shafan the Scribe held an especially honored position and served three successive kings of Judah: Josiah, Johoiakim and Zedekiah. Another

---

[1] Y. Aharoni, *Arad Inscriptions* (Jerusalem, 1981), Inscriptions Nos. 4, 10, 13, 17.

[2] D. Diringer, "Early Hebrew Inscriptions," in Olga Tufnell, *Lachish* III (London, 1953), 348.

[3] N. Avigad, "The Epitaph of the Royal Steward from Siloam Village," *IEJ* 3 (1953), 137-152.

renowned scribe was Baruch son of Neriah, who was close to the prophet Jeremiah, whom he served as a scribe. A bulla stamped with his full name "Berekhiahu son of Neriyahu, the scribe"[4] was found recently among a group of more than 200 bullae. Among the recent additions to the seals of scribes is the Hebrew seal of "M'S son of Manoah the scribe."[5]

SERVANT OF THE KING, עבד המלך . This title appears only twice in the Bible, both times in connection with Asayah. His functions are not specified, but it is obvious that he was a high-ranking functionary close to the king (2 Kings 22:12). The title "servant of the king" is also mentioned in one of the Lachish letters. So far, a relatively large number of seals have been found bearing the title "servant of the king," or "servant" followed by the name of the king. Some originate in Israel and Judah, mentioning the kings Jeroboam (Pl. XI-1), Uzziah, Ahaz and Hezekiah, while others are from the neighboring countries of Ammon, Philistia (Ashkelon) and Phoenicia (Byblos).

SON OF THE KING, בן המלך . In the Bible, five persons bear this title. Although descendants of the king, apparently they did not occupy the highest positions in the state. Joash, Jerahmeel and Malkiah were connected with the prison and took part in the imprisonment of the prophet Jeremiah, and of Baruch the Scribe. A large number of seals and bullae carrying the title "son of the king" are known, and recently the title "daughter of the king" has been found on the seal of Ma'adana, daughter of the king.[6]

SERVANT, נער . The term "servant" (na'ar) is used several times in the Bible in the sense of a household manager or personal attendant (1 Sam. 2:13), or in other cases, in the sense of armor-bearer (2 Sam. 18:15). The plural "servants" (ne'arim) has at times a military connotation (Neh. 4:10). The title also appears in the seal impression of Elyaqim, servant of Yaukin, on a number of pottery jar-handles,[7] which were all impressed with the same seal (Pl. XI-2).

GOVERNOR OF THE CITY, שר העיר . The governor of the city (sar ha'ir) was responsible for the municipal administration. The title is mentioned several times in the Bible, as in the case of Amon, governor of Samaria (1 Kings 22:26) and Maaseiah, governor of Jerusalem (2 Chron. 34:8). The title (שר ער), written in defective spelling and without a definite article, is incised on several jars from Kuntillet 'Ajrud,[8] which date from about 800 B.C.E. The title, written with the definite article (שר העיר) on two identical bullae[9] from the end of the First Temple period, probably refers to Jerusalem.

CHIEF OF THE CORVÉE, אשר על המס . The Israelites took over the corvée system from the Canaanites and after the establishment of the monarchy, the corvée became a state-organized institution. A seal,[10] which dates from the 7th century, is the only clear extra-biblical evidence of the practice of mas (corvée) in Israel.

[4] N. Avigad, "Baruch The Scribe and Jerahmeel The King's Son," *IEJ* 28 (1978), 52-56.

[5] P. Bordreuil, "Inscriptions sigillaires ouest—sémitiques, II: un cachet récemment acquis par le Cabinet des médailles de la Bibliothèque Nationale," *Syria* 52 (1975), 197-118.

[6] N. Avigad, "The King's Daughter and the Lyre," *IEJ* 28 (1978), 146-151.

[7] W. F. Albright, "King Joiachim in Exile," *BiAr* 5 (Dec. 1942), 49-55; Y. Aharoni, *Excavations at Ramat Rahel, Preliminary report, seasons 1961 and 1962* (Rome, 1964), p. 33; see also D. Ussishkin, "Royal Judean Storage Jars and Private Seal Impressions," *BASOR* 223 (1976), 6-13.

[8] Z. Meshel, *Kuntillet 'Ajrud: a religious centre from the time of the Judaean monarchy on the border of Sinai*, Israel Museum Catalogue 175 (Jerusalem, 1978).

[9] N. Avigad, "The Governor of The City," *IEJ* 26 (1976), 178-182.

[10] N. Avigad, "The Chief of the Corvée," *IEJ* 80 (1980), 170-173.

"PRIVATE" SEALS OF OFFICE HOLDERS. To the group of seals of public office-holders should be added a large number of seals and seal-impressions bearing the names of their owner without any title. Three seals inscribed with the name Elyashib son of Eshiyahu[11] (Pl. XI-3) were discovered in the excavations of the fortress of Arad in a room next to the archives, where many ostraca addressed to Elyashib were found. These seals are of great importance because this is the first time that seals have been found in the place where they had been used, and that we have some information concerning their owner and the time in which he lived. At Arad, it is clear that these "private" seals, which bear only their owner's name without a title, in fact belonged to the commander of the fortress. The ostraca addressed to Elyashib indicate that he was in charge of the stores of oil, wine and flour. The royal fortress at Arad served as an administrative center for the region, and essential commodities were issued from its stores to various military units which passed through Arad. The existence of three seals bearing Elyashib's name may indicate that his subordinates had the authority to use his seal. From Arad ostracon No. 17 we learn the name of another official who had a seal of his own for sealing official dispatches: "To Nahum, (and) now: go to the house of Elyashib son of Eshyahu and take from there one (jar of) oil, and send it to Ziph quickly and seal it with your seal."[12] On the reverse, we read: "on the 24th of the month Nahum gave oil into the hand of the Kitti. . . ." The conclusion that seals bearing names without titles are not necessarily "private" seals is important for our understanding of the significance of the "private" seal impressions found on store-jar handles together with *lamelekh* seal impressions (Pl. XI-4).

Hundreds of jar-handles bearing *lamelekh* stamps have been found in Judaean sites. The oval impressions are divided into three registers: Above appears the word *lamelekh*, "belonging to the king" and below the name of one of four towns—Hebron, Socoh, Ziph or MMŠT; in the middle register is a symbol, a winged scarab or a winged scroll or sun-disc. These impressions are generally held to have been stamped by royal officials as a guarantee of the capacity of the store-jars. Another view regards these store-jars as being intended for taxes in kind—oil or wine—and the four towns mentioned in the sealings as administrative centers in Judah, where the taxes were gathered. Still another view holds them to be wine-jars, and the official seals on their handles would then denote the place of origin of the wine. Recent excavations at Lachish[13] provide us with new data concerning the royal Judean store-jars. Ten jars with royal seal-impressions were completely restored, as well as about the same number of unstamped jars, all coming from Level III. One of the jars has all four of its handles stamped, two with אחמלך משלם and two with למלך שכה. The liquid capacity of the jars which were measured ranges between 43.00 and 51.80 litres. The average capacity is around 45 litres (two baths?) but the difference in volume, which comes to 8.80 litres, leads us to reconsider the suggestion that the royal stamps were a guarantee of capacity. Unstamped store-jars of Type 484 (according to Tufnell's classification)[14] are very common and were frequently discovered in the same locus as the stamped jars. Many of them are similar to the stamped jars in shape, size, material and color, thus establishing another class of royal Judean store-jars. These are

[11] Aharoni, *op. cit.* (above, n.1), 119.

[12] *Ibid.*, Inscription No. 17.

[13] Ussishkin, *op. cit.* (above, n.7), 1-13; *Idem*, "Lachish in the Days of the Kingdom of Judah—The Recent Archaeological Excavations," *Qadmoniot* 15, 2-3 (1982), 50-51 (Hebrew).

[14] Olga Tufnell, *Lachish* III *The Iron Age* (London, 1953), 315-316, Pl. 95:464.

very common in Level III at Lachish and are completely absent from the sealed deposits of Level II.

On purely archaeological grounds, as Ussishkin showed,[15] it is quite clear that the royal and private stamps were connected. First, the handles with private stamps are similar in type to the handles of the royal store-jars. Second, the distribution of the handles with private stamps matches that of the royal stamps. Moreover, private stamps have been found together with *lamelekh* stamps in various sites, and in some cases, handles with the same private stamp were discovered at different sites. According to Tufnell[16] and Ussishkin,[17] Level III of Lachish was destroyed by Sennacherib in 701 B.C.E. Lemaire[18] came to the conclusion that by palaeographical criteria, the royal seal-impressions of all classes can be dated to the 8th century B.C.E. Nadav Na'aman[19] suggested that storage jars with *lamelekh* stamps should be connected with Hezekiah's preparations in anticipation of an Assyrian campaign against Judah prior to 701 B.C.E. The dispersal of *lamelekh* stamps corresponds perfectly to the kingdom of Hezekiah in its western and northern limits. The last contributors to the discussion, Perlman and his colleagues,[20] analyzed 118 *lamelekh*-type jar-handles, which included some with private stamps and some without any stamps at all. They used the Neutron Activation Analysis technique, which permits the accurate measurement of wide array of chemical elements, most of which are present only in the parts-per-million range. The provenience can be ascertained only if it is known to which specific site the composition of the clay belongs. The chemical analyses show a degree of homogeneity of composition which is normally associated with pottery made at a single site and it can be said without serious doubt that the site lies in the Shephelah.

The conclusion seems clearly warranted that the four place-names which appear on the *lamelekh* stamps are not related to the place where the jars were produced. The evidence concerning the provenience of the *lamelekh* jars gives support to the idea that there was a central pottery-making center which was assigned the task of making all these containers.

Perlman's conclusions strengthen the assumption of De Vaux,[21] Demski,[22] and others, that the Judaean Achzib mentioned in Micha 1 was a manufacturing center which housed potters who were in the king's service and produced vessels for the royal court. Potters also worked in Netaim and Gedera (1 Chronicles 4:21-3).

In conclusion, a number of questions are left unanswered. If we assume that all the jars carrying the four place-names were made in the same pottery workshop, what was the function of the persons mentioned in the "private" seal-impressions? Were they potters, or officials responsible for the capacity of the jars or for the whole process of production and distribution? Did the jars contain wine or oil? From the Arad inscriptions it seems

---

[15] Ussishkin, *op. cit.* (above n.7), 3.

[16] Tufnell, *op. cit.* (above, n.14), 55-56.

[17] D. Ussishkin, "The destruction of Lachish by Sennacherib and the dating of the Royal Judean storage jars," *Tel Aviv* 4 (1977), 28-60.

[18] A. Lemraire, "Remarques sur la datation des estampilles '*lmlk*,'" *Vetus Testamentum* 25 (1975), 680.

[19] N. Na'aman, "Sennacherib's campaign to Judah and the Date of the *LMLK* stamps," *Vetus Testamentum* 29 (1979), 60-86.

[20] H. Mommsen, I. Perlman, J. Yellin, "On the Provenience of the LMLK jars," The Hebrew University Jerusalem, Laboratory for Archaeometry, Institute of Archaeology and Faculty of Science, *HUAL* 12 (1981), 1-25 and tables.

[21] R. de Vaux, *Ancient Israel, its Life and Institutions* (London, 1961), 76-78.

[22] A. Demsky, "The 'Houses of Achzib' (A Critical Note on Micha 1:14b)," *IEJ* 16 (1966), 211-215.

that the main provisions kept in the storehouses of the strongholds were flour, oil, and wine. Among the cities fortified by Rehoboam in Judah, which are listed in 2 Chronicles 11:5-10, are Socoh, Ziph and Hebron, three of the four towns appearing in the *lamelekh* stamps. The chapter continues: "And he fortified the strongholds and put captains in them, and stores of food and of oil and wine." It might well be that the royal pottery workshops produced a large number of jars at one time, and that each batch of jars was stamped by the official in charge with the royal seal, bearing the name of only one of the four cities, who then added his own seal. Only some of the handles in each consignment were stamped to indicate their destination; then the jars were shipped to be filled with oil or wine, depending on the commodity the city specialized in, or perhaps on the specific responsibility of the official. From there the jars were sent to the various strongholds, to be used by the military forces in times of emergency.

Returning to the seal impressions, we can see that the letters on many of them are crude and uneven, resembling the inscriptions found on seals made of local hard limestone.[23] It can be assumed that some of these seals were made on the spot for the official by someone who was not an expert gem-cutter, though he must have been literate.

A detailed list of functionaries is found in 1 Chronicles 27:25-31, which records the officials responsible for the various branches of the economy, mainly farming (although it is attributed by the Chronicler to David's time, this administrative framework reflects the time of Hezekiah).[24]

[23] *IS*, Nos. 22-25, 62, 71, 81.

[24] Sarah Japhet, *The Ideology of the Book of Chronicles and its Place in Biblical Thought* (Jerusalem, 1977), 333 (Hebrew).

THE SEAL OF MIQNÊYAW, SERVANT OF YAHWEH*

FRANK MOORE CROSS

Harvard University

1

The seal of Miqnêyaw is no doubt the most interesting and important piece in the collection of inscribed Hebrew seals belonging to the Harvard Semitic Museum. According to a reliable report I have reason to believe, it was found in a tomb in the vicinity of Jerusalem. It is exquisitely designed and engraved on a highly polished piece of red jasper mottled with veins of white jasper. It is ellipsoid in shape and unusually delicate in size: 11.5 x 7.5 x 4.5 mm.[1] The seal is bored through with a longitudinal perforation. Save for its inscriptions, the seal is devoid of all ornamentation. There is neither a border around the seal nor the familiar double lines separating the lines of script. Such austere simplicity is excessively rare in seals of this date, and stands in striking contrast to the ornate seals of Judean officials of the eighth century B.C.E.[2]

Both sides of the seal bear legends. On one side, which we shall label the obverse, it is engraved with the script in the positive so as to be read directly; on the other side it is engraved in the negative for use in sealing. On the obverse the inscription reads in two lines:

mqnyw
'bd.yḥwh

On the reverse it is also inscribed in two lines:

lmqnyw
'bd.yhwh
"(Belonging) to Miqnêyaw
Servant of Yahweh"

Appropriately the l- of possession is used only on the side designed for making *bullae*. In both inscriptions we note particularly the use of the word-divider separating the words

---

*For Professor Nachman Avigad, in homage.

[1] One may compare the small, ellipsoid seal of *yrmyhw* (Avigad, *EI* 9, No. 14; *IS* 45) from the early or mid-eighth century B.C.E. measures 9 x 7 x 5 mm and is of similar fine craftsmanship.

[2] See, for example, the seals of the officials of Jeroboam (*IS* 3), Uzziah (Diringer XXI, 2 and 4), and 'Ahaz (Moscati XII, 9). On the other hand compare the plain, inscribed seal of Yahūzaraḥ the official of Hezekiah (*IS* 4).

'ebed and *yahweh*. It is clear that *'ebed. yahweh* is the title of Miqnêyaw, not his patronymic. A name formed with the full tetragrammaton would in any case be unique and accordingly unacceptable in the Hebrew onomasticon. The unexpected word-divider certifies the reading as a title.

The occurrence of the divine name in this seal is its first authentic appearance on a Hebrew seal.[3] As a matter of fact, before the recent discoveries at Kuntillet 'Ajrūd in Sinai, it was the earliest occurrence in a native Israelite inscription.[4] The owner's name, Miqnêyaw, is well known in its variant form *mqnyhw/miqnêyāhû/*. It occurs as a name of a musician and singer in a list of twelve famous singers of early Israel in 1 Chronicles 15, 18.21.[5] A seal of the early seventh century B.C.E. bears the name *lmqnyhw [b]n yhwmlk*.[6] The name may be taken to mean "the creature of Yahweh," or the "property of Yahweh," probably the former, the root *qny* carrying its archaic force as in such divine epithets as *'ēl qōnê 'arṣ*, "'El creator of earth."[7]

2

The beautiful and characteristic script of the Miqnêyaw seal has its closest parallels in the scripts of seals of the first half of the eighth century B.C.E.: the seal of *šm' 'bd yrb'm* (ca. 783-745),[8] the seal of *šbnyw 'bd 'zyw* and *'byw 'bd 'zyw* (ca. 768-734),[9] the seal of *šmryw*,[10] the seal of *yrmyhw*,[11] and the seal of *'šyw bn ywqm/'aśayaw bin yawqīm/*.[12] The script of the Samaria Ostraca from the years 778-774 B.C.E.,[13] and the Hebrew script of the Nimrud Ivory[14] from the early eighth century also stand very close to that of the Miqnêyaw seal. On the other hand, the script of the seals of *'šn' 'bd 'ḥz* (ca. 734-715 B.C.E.)[15] and *yhwzrḥ bn ḥlqyhw 'bd ḥzqyhw* (ca. 715-687 B.C.E.)[16] are distinctly later as is the script of the Samaria Barley Check (from before 722 B.C.E.).

---

[3] The name, indeed the epithet *'bd yhwh*, does appear on the "seal of David," a notorious forgery of the last century. See Diringer, 320 f., and the bibliography cited.

[4] On the inscriptions from Kuntillet 'Ajrūd which date from ca. 825-800, see provisionally Z. Meshel, *Kuntillet 'Ajrud: A Religious Center from the Jewish Monarchy on the Border of Sinai* (Jerusalem, Israel Museum, 1978). For a discussion of the earliest non-Israelite occurrence of the divine name, see F. M. Cross, *Canaanite Myth and Hebrew Epic* (Cambridge, Harvard University Press, 1973), 61f.

[5] We follow the scholarly consensus in reading *hmšnym* in 1 Chronicles 15, 18 *šnym 'śr*.

[6] Moscati XIV, 8. See also *mqnyhw* in the 'Arad ostraca: Y. Aharoni, *Arad Inscriptions* (Jerusalem, Israel Exploration Society, 1981), No. 60, 4 and 72, 1. Aharoni reads *nknyhw* in the latter case, but the name better conforms to *mqnyhw* as pointed out to me by R. B. Lawton.

[7] For references and discussion, see F. M. Cross, *Canaanite Myth and Hebrew Epic*, 16, n.20 and 50f. and n.25; and P. D. Miller, "El, the Creator of Earth," *BASOR* 239 (1980), 43-46.

[8] *IS* 3.

[9] Diringer XXI, 4 and XXI, 2.

[10] *IS* 35.

[11] See above, n.1.

[12] Diringer XX, 8. It should be noted that the drawing and description in Diringer is superior to more recent ones.

[13] On these dates, see F. M. Cross, "Ammonite Ostraca from Heshbon," *Andrews University Seminary Studies* 13 (1975), 8-10 and n.24.

[14] See A. R. Millard, "Alphabetic Inscriptions on Ivories from Nimrud," *Iraq* 24 (1962), 41-51 and Pl. XXIV, A.

[15] C. C. Torrey, "A Hebrew Seal from the Reign of Ahaz," *BASOR* 79 (1940), 27f. and Fig. 1.

[16] *IS* 4.

The script of the seal of ʿAśayaw ben Yawqīm is particularly close in typology to that of the seal of Miqnêyaw. It must be stressed that this seal dates to the early or at latest mid-8th century and that the *yawqīm* of the seal cannot be identified with *yĕhôyaqīm* (older *yahûyāqīm*) king of Judah in the years 609-598 B.C.E. This is clear on several lines of evidence including palaeographical and linguistic, pertinent both to its dating, the dating of the Miqnêyaw seal, and to the dating of the famous seal of ʾElyaqīm steward (*náʿar*) of Yawkīn. In the first place, there is the use in these seals of the syncopated form of the divine name *-yaw*. So far as our evidence goes, this form does not appear in Judah in the age of the monarchy after the 8th century.[17] All Hebrew seals from Northern Israel use *-yaw-*,[18] and the same is true of ostraca of northern provenience. In Judah *-yhw-/yahû/* was used in the 8th century, and, as well, in a small group of seals, including seals of officials of Jerusalem, the syncopated form *-yaw-* appears: *ʾbyw ʿbd ʿzyw, šbnyw ʿbd ʿzyw, mqnyw ʿbd yhwh, ʾlyqm nʿr ywkn, ʾśyw bn ywqm,* and *ʿzryw hgbh.*[19] In Judah in the 7th-6th centuries *-yhw-/yahû/* is used exclusively. That the form *-yhw-/yahû/* was pronounced with the *h* sounded (and hence not merely historical spelling) is clear from Babylonian transcriptions of the early 6th century B.C.E.[20] The Weidner texts include striking examples of the name of Jehoiachin (king of Judah): ¹Ya-ku-ú-ki-nu/*yahûkīn*/, and ya-ʾ-ú-DU/*yahûkīn*/.[21] The Murašû texts also include several names in which the *h* of *yahû* (in the initial position) is written with *ḫ*, for example, ᴵᵈ ya-ḫu-ú-na-ta-nu/*yahûnatan*/.[22] The names *yawqīm* and *yawkīn* are haplological reductions, presumably caritatives, of the longer forms *yawyaqīm* and *yawyakīn*. In the 7th and 6th centuries the Judean

---

[17] The form *yaw* develops in the Judaean dialect in the late 6th or early 5th century, first apparently in the final position, on 5th century stamps (*ʾwryw,zbdyw*) and in late 6th and 5th century Babylonian transcriptions (*-ya-a-ma* reflecting *-yaw*). In the 5th century *yaw-* is also found sporadically in the initial position alongside forms written *yhw*. In the course of the 4th century *yaw* contracted to *yô*, leading to the hypercorrected form *yĕhô-*. See F. M. Cross, *Canaanite Myth and Hebrew Epic*, 65, N. 78; M. D. Coogan, *West Semitic Personal Names in the Murašû Documents*. HSM 7 (Missoula, Montana, Scholars Press, 1976), 49-53 [several dates for seals must be corrected in his discussion, see below]; N. Avigad, *Bullae and Seals from a Post-Exilic Judean Archive*. Qedem 4 (Jerusalem, The Hebrew University, 1976), 22; and "Seals of Exiles" *IEJ* 15 (1965), 230 ff. and Pl. 40F.

[18] *yaw* is used both in initial and final positions in these Northern names.

[19] The last-mentioned seal, which I should date no later than the mid-8th century B.C.E. was published by N. Avigad, "A Seal with a Family Emblem" *IEJ* 16 (1966), 50-53. Noteworthy are the archaic *hes* with long "legs" and the top horizontal stopping flush with the vertical leg (i.e., not breaking through to the right). Other seals apparently from Judah bearing *-yaw-* elements include the following: from Hebron (?) comes *ywʿr* from ca. 700 B.C.E. (Avigad *EI* 9 [1969]; No. 15); from Ramat Raḥel and Jerusalem *ywbnh* (*IR* 89) from the late 8th century (another seal of *mnḥm/ywbnh* of which sealings are known from Ramat Raḥel and Beth-shemesh appears to have been miswritten and secondarily corrected to *yhwbnh* [Herr 52]); acquired in Jerusalem, two seals bearing the names *ywʿš* (Avigad, *BIES* 19 [1954], No. 5) and *ywʾmn* (Avigad, *BIES* 18 [1954], No. 6) both crudely written and hence difficult to date, but probably of the late 8th century B.C.E. From Murabbaʿât in a papyrus of ca. 700 B.C.E. (on this dating see the discussion in the paper cited above N. 13) comes the name *ywʿzr* (*IR* 32).

[20] The interpretation of these data was developed jointly by the writer and Robert B. Lawton in a preliminary study for his dissertation "Israelite Personal Names on Hebrew Inscriptions Antedating 500 B.C.E." (unpublished dissertation, Harvard University, 1977).

[21] E. F. Weidner "Jojachin, König von Juda, in babylonischen Keilschrifttexten," *Mélanges syriens offerts à Monsieur René Dussaud* (Paris, Paul Geuthner, 1939) II, 923-928.

[22] See M. D. Coogan in the work cited above, n.17, p. 27f.

hapological forms of these names were *yahûkîn*, properly written *yhwkn*, and *yahûqim*, written *yhwqm*. *Yhwkn*, as it happens, is not extant as a Judaean seal, though this form is reflected precisely in the Weidner transcriptions; *yhwqm* actually appears on two seals.[23]

The occasional appearance of the element -*yaw*- in Judah on seals of the 8th century including seals of royal officials before the time of Hezekiah requires explanation. It is clear that the normal theophorous element was *yhw* pronounced *yahû* in Judah generally. Its exclusive use in names of the 7th-6th centuries, and its transcription in cuneiform suggests or even requires that the writing *yhw* arose in late Judah not from a restoration of historical spelling, but reflected the actual pronunciation -*yahû*-. I should suggest that in the Judaean court dialect of the 8th century, the pronunciation *yaw*, characteristic of the Israelite court in the North was affected, but was supplanted by the "rustic" dialect of Judah from the time of Hezekiah onward. Such an affectation or court dialect would not be surprising. The Israelite and Judaean royal houses were mingled from the days of the dominant Omrides. Of the two, Judah was the more rustic kingdom until the fall of Samaria in 722 B.C.E. One may compare the struggle between the court language of Norway derived from Danish (Riksmål) and the common Norse dialect of the Norwegian folk (Landsmål).[24]

In short, on linguistic-onomastic grounds alone the seals of *'šyw bn ywqm* and *'lyqm n'r ywkn* belong to the 8th century B.C.E. and do not fit into the onomastic patterns of Judah in the 7th or 6th century. Even stronger is the evidence of palaeography, and it was the palaeographical evidence that first forced me to argue for an 8th century date for the 'Elyaqîm steward of Yawkín sealings found at Tell Beit Mirsim, Ramat Raḥel, and Beth-shemesh.[25] No letter in the seal's inscription need be later than the end of the 8th century, and the *waw* in particular is archaic, comparable to the *waw*s of the Nimrud Ivory and the Samaria Ostraca. Professor Nachman Avigad has demonstrated that the element *ná'ar*, "steward," need not, indeed often was not, the title of a royal officer, clearing away one of W. F. Albright's strongest arguments for identifying *Yawkîn* with king Jehoiachin.[26] More recently, David Usshishkin has demonstrated that the *'Elyaqîm ná'ar Yawkîn* sealings must be associated with the *lam-mélek* or royal Judaean stamps, and that both appear in Lachish, Level III, which came to an end in 701 B.C.E.[27]

The comparison of the seal of *Maqnêyaw 'ébed Yahweh* with the seals of *'aśayaw ben yawqîm* and *šûbnayaw 'ébed 'uzzîyaw* reveal other interesting features in common. All

---

[23] The seal of *yhwqm* (Avigad, *EI* 12 [1975], No. 12 from the 8th century B.C.E., and *yhwqm/yhwndb* (Avigad, *EI* 12 [1975], No. 13. One may compare also the similar haplological form *yhwkl/yahûkal/* (from Yahûyûkal) found in two Judaean seals (*IR* 27 from Lachish, and Herr 63 from Tell eṣ-Ṣâfî).

[24] See Einar Haugen, *Language Conflict and Language Planning: The Case of Modern Norwegian* (Cambridge, Harvard University Press, 1966).

[25] My views of the linguistic and palaeographic evidence requiring a raising of the date of the *'Elyaqîm ná'ar Yawkîn* seal were first presented in a paper delivered to the World Congress of Jewish Studies, August 15, 1973. Cf. A. Malamat, "The Twilight of Judah: In the Egyptian-Babylonian Maelstrom," *Vetus Testamentum Supplement* 28 (1975), 138, n.34.

[26] N. Avigad, "New Light on the Na'ar Seals," *Magnalia Dei*. G. E. Wright Volume, ed. F. M. Cross, W. E. Lemke, and P. D. Miller (New York, Doubleday, 1976), 294-300. W. F. Albright's influential paper, "The Seals of Eliakim and the Latest Pre-Exilic History of Judah," *JBL* 51 (1932), 77-106, has been crucial in fixing both the political and archaeological chronology of Judah. If the linchpin—the date of the Eliakim seal—is removed, as it must be, the repercussions are not inconsiderable.

[27] David Ussishkin, "Royal Judean Storage Jars and Private Seal Impressions," *BASOR* 223 (1976), 1-13; and "The Destruction of Lachish by Sennacherib and the Dating of the Royal Judean Storage Jars" *Tel Aviv* 4 (1977), 28-60.

three are engraved on two sides, a rare trait in this corpus of Hebrew seals. The Miqnêyaw seal has script on both sides; the 'Aśayaw seal has script on one side and decorations, including the sun child, Horus, sitting on a lotus, (popular on 9th-century Phoenician ivories), on the other;[28] the Šubnayaw seal has script and decorations on both sides. Both the Miqnêyaw seal and the Šubnayaw seal appear to have been made of a similar, if not identical, rare stone: red jasper with white veins.[29]

It is by palaeographical analysis, however, that we can best fix the date of the Miqnêyaw seal. The evidence, as we shall see, points to a date in the first half of the 8th century B.C.E. In analyzing the typology of the script I shall follow the order of the letters in the inscriptions.

Lamed is made with a bold, rounded hook and relatively long arm. It is a form which characterizes the 8th century cursive and lapidary scripts, for example, the Samaria Ostraca and the *l'šyw bn ywqm* seal. The form dies out in the cursive scripts in the 7th century, but persists in slightly modified form—sporadically—in lapidary scripts. It is therefore of little diagnostic value.

The *mem* is a variant of the "double-check" *mem* in which the second stroke of the first (left) check is vestigial. It is a form primarily found in the glyptic of the 8th century, though a nearly identical form appears sporadically in the Samaria Ostraca and in the so-called Name List (C1012) of Samaria.[30] The closest parallels to the Miqnêyaw *mem* are found on the *šm' 'bd yrb'm* seal (the second *mem*), the *šmryw* seal, and the *yrmyhw* seal. The *mem* is less developed than the Siloam *mem*, in which the second and fourth strokes (the right sides originally of the "double check") have tended toward the horizontal.

Qop is preserved in two forms with slightly differing heads. One is egg-shaped, an archaic form typologically known elsewhere in Hebrew only in texts from Kuntillet 'Ajrûd (cf. the *qop* of the Mesha' Stone). The other *qop* is flattened on the bottom of the left side of the head, a form found in 'Aśayaw seal, and in the Samaria Ostraca. One should note, however, that the vertical leg extends up to the top of the head, unlike the more developed cursive *qop* of the Samaria Ostraca, the Siloam inscription, and later texts.

Nun shows little typological development in the 9th, 8th, and 7th centuries B.C.E., and cannot be used for dating, but the *yod* of *Yahweh* on the obverse is characterized by a characteristic downward tick in the right end of the long tail. We can trace this form from the Kuntillet 'Ajrûd texts from the end of the 9th century into early 8th century inscriptions: the Nimrud Ivory, the Šamaryaw seal, the Samaria Ostraca, the 'Aśayaw seal, the Samaria Barley Check, early ostraca from 'Arad, and probably in the *yrmyhw* seal. It disappears in the late 8th century. The tendency to make a downward tick on the final horizontal stroke of letters marks the emergence of a series of peculiarly Hebrew letter-forms beginning in the late 9th century B.C.E.: on *'alep* (surviving sporadically into the 6th century), on *zayin* (it is regular as long as the Hebrew script survived), on *yod* (dying out in the second half of the 8th century), *samek* and *ṣade* (regular as long as the script lived). This tendency operated both north and south, in Israel and Judah.

---

[28] The Horus child on the flower is also found on the contemporary seal of *'abīyaw 'ébed 'uzzīyaw*.

[29] I hope in the future to examine the *šubnayaw 'ébed 'uzzīyaw* seal. At present I am dependent on non-technical, published descriptions.

[30] See S. A. Birnbaum in *The Objects from Samaria. Samaria Sebaste* III (London), *PEF*, 1957), 17f.; Pl. I-4; and F. M. Cross, "Epigraphic Notes on the Hebrew Documents of the Eighth-Sixth Centuries II," *BASOR* 165 (1962), 35, n.7. I refer to the *mem* in *mn[ḥm]* 1.5.

The *waw* has an "open" head identical with forms from Kuntillet ʿAjrūd, the Nimrud Ivory, the Samaria Ostraca, and the *ʾElyaqim náʿar Yawkīn* seal. The right oblique stroke breaks through the vertical only slightly to the left, and the left oblique hooks only slightly. In the *waw* of *yhwh* on the reverse, it has no hook, comparable to the *waw* of the *yrmyhw* seal.

The *ʿayin* is relatively large, high and rhomboidal in shape, very like the form on the *ʾAśayaw* seal.

Bet is short-legged and formal. The elongated, narrow *bet* which appears as early as the Samaria Ostraca has not influenced its form. Identical are the *bets* on the *ʿbd yrbʿm* seal and the *šbnyw ʿbd ʿzyw* seal.

Dalet is an important letter palaeographically. In the early 8th century the right line of the triangle breaks through downward to form a leg. The breakthrough is found already in the Samaria Ostraca, and in both the *ʿebed ʿuzzīyaw* seals, and in the *ʿebed ʾaḥaz* has become quite long. *Dalet* remains a perfect triangle in the *ʿAjrūd* Stone Bowl, the Nimrud Ivory, and in the *šmʿ ʿbd yrbʿm* seal. One example from the Miqnêyaw seal (on the reverse) is a perfect triangle without breakthrough. The *dalet* on the reverse has a minute breakthrough comparable to that of the *ʿAjrūd* cursive and the Samaria Ostraca. A second development begins in the 8th century, a breakthrough upward of the top line of the *dalet*, comparable to the contemporary breakthrough of the top stroke of *he*. It is found in rudimentary development sporadically in the Samaria Ostraca, and is full-blown in the script of Siloam. No trace of this feature is found in the Miqnêyaw seal.

He is long-legged—an 8th century trait. More important, the top horizontal exhibits no tendency to break through the vertical to the right. This archaic, classical *he* is found at ʿAjrūd, in the *zryw hgbh* seal, and the *ldlh* seal.[31] On the other hand, the tendency to "breakthrough" is full developed already in the Samaria Ostraca and Barley Check.

These typological features of the script of the *ʾÉbed Yahwah* seal form a cluster of consistent archaic traits pointing to a date in the first half of the 8th century B.C.E.

3

The title *ʿebed yahweh* which Miqnêyaw claims is, of course, one of the elements of chief interest in this unique seal.[32] Literally volumes have been written on the title *ʿebed yahweh* in the Hebrew Bible, and especially on the use and meaning of this title in the oracles of Second Isaiah.[33] When the expression *ʿebed yahweh* is used as a *terminus technicus*, what does it mean, or to whom does it refer? In recent years many scholars have insisted that it is primarily a royal title. David or the son of David is peculiarly the *ʿebed yahweh*. Kirta in

---

[31] See Avigad, *EI* 9 (1969), No. 4. This seal which shares with the two *ʿebed ʿUzzīyaw* seals and the ʾAśayaw seal the motif of the child Horus on the lotus is to be dated to the early or mid-8th century. Both *hē* and *dalet* are archaic.

[32] Names following the pattern *ʿbd*+DN, "slave of DN," are very common in Hebrew and other West Semitic onomastica. We do not propose to examine these here. For a recent discussion and bibliography, see Michael Silverman, "Servant (ʿebed) Names in Aramaic and in the Other Semitic Languages," *JAOS* 101 (1981), 361-366.

[33] Convenient summaries and bibliography may be found in W. Zimmerli's article παις θεου in *ThW_z NT* also published in separate form in W. Zimmerli and J. Jeremias, *The Servant of God*. SBT 20 (Napierville, Illinois, Allenson, 1957); C. Lindhagen, *The Servant Motif in the Old Testament* (Uppsala, 1950); and C. R. North, *The Suffering Servant in Deutero-Isaiah*, 2nd ed. (Oxford, Oxford University Press, 1956).

the Ugaritic royal epic is the *'abdu 'ili*.[34] It has been claimed—falsely—that Azitawadda of Danūna who bears the title *'abd ba'l* was king of the Danunites.[35] In short, excessive energy has been exerted to limit the office of the *'ébed yahweh*, and hence the so-called Suffering Servant of Second Isaiah, to that of the royal office and conceptions stemming from Canaanite and Israelite royal ideology and its technical vocabulary. Thus, although it is obvious that prophets and various cultic functionaires may be called *'abdê yahweh*, "slaves/ servants of Yahweh"—as may simple worshippers—the argument has been pressed that originally the formal title applied to the royal office, to the son of David.

In view of this discussion of the Hebrew title *'ébed yahweh*, it is not impertinent to examine contemporary West Semitic seals bearing the simple epithet *'ébed* plus divine name: *'bd. DN*. To my knowledge there are four such seals extant. There is, first of all, *Miqnêyaw 'ébed yahweh*, obviously not a king of Judah (or Israel). There is the Ammonite seal which must be read *ltmk'l ['*]*bd mlkm*, "(Belonging) to Tamak'el servant of Milkom."[36] *Tamak'el* a figure of the 6th century B.C. has no claim on the royal office of 'Ammon. Thanks to the discovery of the Tell Sīrān Inscription we can now fill in all, or virtually all, of the kings of 'Ammon from ca. 700 to the end of the kingdom toward 580 B.C.E.[37] An early Aramaic seal, roughly contemporary with the Miqnêyaw seal, bears the legend *ḥtm brq 'bd/'tršmn*, "the seal of Baraq, slave of 'Attaršamên."[38] The script exhibits traits we associate with Trans-Jordanian traditions of Aramaic, and the god bears a favorite epithet of a North-Arabian league. Baraq may well be an Aramaized Arab. It is highly unlikely that he was a king. A fourth seal, a beautifully engraved piece from Trans-Jordan, written in a curiously Hebraizing script of the late 8th or early 7th century B.C.E., is inscribed: *šmš'zr/'bd šhr*, "Šamš'azar, slave of Šahr.[39] It is not impossible that the second line be read *'bdšhr*, a personal name, and is the patronymic of Šamš-'azar; no word divider separates the words. In any case Šamš'azar, if a king, is as yet unknown.[40]

In the era before the Israelite kingdom there are references in cuneiform documents found in Syria-Palestine to persons entitled *marad DN*, "servant of DN" or *amat DN*, "maid-servant of DN."[41] In particular there are a number of cylinder seals found in Syria-Palestine and in Egypt belonging to the 18th-15th centuries B.C.E. (roughly contemporary with the old Babylonian Period in Mesopotamia) which bear inscriptions giving the personal name of the owner, often his or her occupation, and the expression *marad DN* or *amat*

---

[34] *CTA* 14.3.153 and 14.6.299/300.

[35] *KAI* 26, I. 1/2. The key phrase is found in I.11 *wyšb 'nk 'l ks' 'by* "and I set him (the scion of my lord, *srš 'dny* of 1.10) on the throne of his father." The phrase can be vocalized *wa-yôšibō 'anōkī 'al kissi' 'abīyū*. cf. J. Friedrich, "Zur interpretation von Satz XVI der phönizische-bildhethitischen Bilinguis von Karatepe," *Or.* 31 (1962), 223f. The Hittite and Phoenician texts combine to suggest that Azitawadda is priest of Ba'l and probably regent of the young son of Urikki ('wrk) king of the Danunites.

[36] See my discussion "Heshbon Ostracon II," *Andrews University Seminary Studies* 11 (1973), 127f., and n.6. The seal is *CIS* II, 94. It has been read *br milkom*, a strange patronymic made more odd by the failure of *mlkm*, an epithet of 'El, to appear in the 'Ammonite onomasticon. The edge of the seal is broken. Earlier I believed I was able to see a trace of an *'ayin*; I am told, however, that broken the edge has obliterated any trace of a letter.

[37] See F. M. Cross, "Notes on the Ammonite Inscription from Tell Sīrān," *BASOR* 212 (1973), 12-15.

[38] Herr 78.

[39] My knowledge of this seal is thanks to Professor Emmett W. Hamrick of Wake Forest University.

[40] Samsi, "queen" of Arabia in this era is, of course, not a candidate in view of the masculine term *'bd*.

[41] Of some interest is Ummaḫnu, the wife of Iškur, maidservant of (the goddess) the Lady of Byblus (*amat bēlit ša Gubla*) mentioned in the letters of Ribaddi, king of Byblus: *TA* 83, 53f.; 84, 42; 86, 24f.

61

DN.[42] There is good reason to believe that these seals conform to Babylonian practice in which the formula, "servant of *DN*" is widely used on cylinder seals and, as Professor William Hallo has pointed out to me, need carry no technical or professional overtones or specifications.

More remotely, we may mention the cultic functionaries at Carthaginian temples who bear the titles *'bd bt 'šmn, 'bd bt 'ršp, 'bd bt mlqrt, 'bd bt 'štrt, 'bd bt šmš,* etc., "slave of the temple of 'Ešmūn, Rešep, Milqqart, Aštart, Šamš.[43]

The data from the West Semitic sources suggest that the formal title *'ébed DN* was used frequently by priestly officials. No doubt each sacral officer, king, prophet, seer, priest, and singer could be termed an *'ébed DN*. It is noteworthy, however, that in inscriptions and seals, a king ordinarily utilized the title "king." The only royal title on Hebrew inscribed seals is *lam-mélek*, "Belonging to the king." And it is not without significance that when the first Hebrew seal with the designation *'ébed yahweh* turns up, the owner proves not to be an Israelite or Judaean king.

4

Who was Miqnêyaw, *'ébed yahweh*? He was not a king. Nor was he a high priest so far as we know, though we must admit that the list of high priests is notoriously defective and incomplete. Moreover, as a king called himself by his royal title, so it appears that high priests called themselves *rab kāhinīma*, "chief of the priests" (Ugarit) "Yôḥanan the priest" (on a Persian-Period coin), or *hak-kōhēn hag-gādōl* (Hasmonaean high priests). On the other hand, the parallels we have drawn, and, it may be added, the aniconic simplicity of the seal combined with its unique elegance, suggest strongly that we are dealing with the seal of a high cultic functionary.

Perhaps we should end our speculating concerning the identity of Miqnêyaw at this point. There is, however, one additional high office in Israel, a cultic official who, according to tradition combined the roles of seer or heirophant with those of musician and singer, and, indeed, rivaled the high priests in dignity and rank.[44] I wonder if Miqnêyaw was not a chief musician in the temple. After all, the one occurrence in the Bible of the name Miqnêyāhû proves to be the name of one of early Israel's famous singers and musicians.[45] Further, in the Psalms, especially in Psalm 135, 1f. and parallel passages, the term *'abdê yahweh* seems

[42] For example an 18th century seal from Beth-shan has the legend: "Mannum the Barū-priest, servant of (the god) Enki." See A. Rowe, *The Topography and History of Beth-shan* (Philadelphia, 1930), Pl. 34,3. From the same era comes a seal of the daughter of the king of Carchemish with the inscription: "Matrunna, daughter of Aplahanda, maidservant of Kubaba." See W. F. Albright, *BASOR* 78 (1940), 26, and *AFO* 5 (1929), 229-231. Other examples may be found in E. Sellin, *Tell Ta'annek I*, (Wien, 1904), 28, Abb. 22; Sidney Smith, "Babylonian Cylinder Seals from Egypt," *JEA* 8 (1922), 207-221 and Pl. XXIII; and G. Dossin, "Le Sceau-cylindre de Dêr-Khabiyeh," *Les annales archéologiques arabes syriennes* 4-5 (1954-55), 39-44.

[43] See F. F. Benz, *Personal Names in the Phoenician and Punic Inscriptions* (Rome, Pontifical Biblical Institute, 1972), 370. These "temple slaves." If such they were, may be compared with the biblical *nᵉtīnīm*.

[44] See the comments on the temple singers in S. Mowinckel, *The Psalms in Israel's Worship*, trans. D. R. Ap-Thomas (Oxford, Basil Blackwell, 1962) II, 81f.; and W. F. Albright, *Archaeology and the Religion of Israel* (Baltimore, Johns Hopkins, 1942), 125-129.

[45] I hasten to say that the Chronicler's attribution of his lists of singers to the time of David is artificial. On the other hand, there is no reason to doubt that his lists do include the names of celebrated singers of

to be narrowed to designate the temple choir, or so it has been argued. Perhaps, therefore, Miqnêyaw the slave of Yahweh was a temple singer, a namesake of the biblical *Miqnêyāhû*. Names tend to repeat in priestly families, Aaronid and Levitic, and, as well, in professional guilds.

These speculations are admittedly precarious. For example, in Brooklyn Papyrus 6, line 7 we read of a certain *Ḥwr ʿbd zy ḥ*[*nwm ʾlh*], "Ḥôr, servant of Hnum, the god." If we had only this passage we could easily propose that he was a high priestly official or one of the famous Egyptian temple singers. However in P. 9, line 10 and P. 10, line 6, this same man is entitled *ḥwr br pṭ ʾsy, gnn zy ḥnwm ʾlh*, "Ḥôr son Peṭeʾisī, gardener of Hnum the god."[46]

In the priestly hierarchy were a number of high officials beneath the chief priest: the "second priest" (*kōhēn mišnê*), the "guardian of the threshold" (*šōmēr has-sap*), the *pāqīd*, "superintendent" in the temple, to name offices mentioned in pre-exile biblical sources. No doubt there were others, by chance unnamed. Miqnêyaw may have held any one of these posts. I must confess, however, that I would find it much more satisfying to picture Miqnêyaw, the servant of Yahweh, not as an unspecified temple functionary, but as a great cantor of early Israel.

---

the age of the First Temple. It may be added that the occurrence of the name *mqnyhw* at ʿArad need not weaken our argument. It has been recognized that a large Levitic contingent flourished at ʿArad, and that traditional names used in priestly of Levitic families abound. After all, it was a temple city as well as military outpost.

[46] E. G. Kraeling, *The Brooklyn Museum Aramaic Papyri.* (New Haven, Yale University Press, 1953).

1. Explusion of Adam and Eve. Pantheon Bible, c. 1150-1175. Trent Museo Diocesano. Photograph after C. R. Dodwell, *Painting in Europe 800 to 1200, Pelican History of Art* (Harmondsworth, 1971) pl. 166.

2. Impression of Syrian cylinder seal in the Seyrig Collection (Seyrig 42). Cabinet des Médailles. Bibliothèque Nationale, Paris. With the kind permission of R. Curiel.

3. Impression of Syrian cylinder seal in the Seyrig Collection (Seyrig 169). Cabinet des Médailles. Bibliothèque Nationale, Paris. With the kind permission of R. Curiel.

4. Impression of Syrian cylinder seal in the Seyrig Collection (Seyrig 142). Cabinet des Médailles. Bibliothèque Nationale, Paris. With the kind permission of R. Curiel.

5. The Harrowing of Hell. Psalter of Hermann von Thuringen. Landesbibliothek, Stuttgart. Photograph after, Otto Demus, *Byzantine Art and the West*, New York 1970, fig. 219.

1a. Scanning micrograph showing one of the collar shapes (arrow) found inside the drill hole of a chalcedony cylinder seal. Similar collars were found on 10 of the 30 crypto crystalline quartz seals ranging from the 1st to the 3rd Millennium

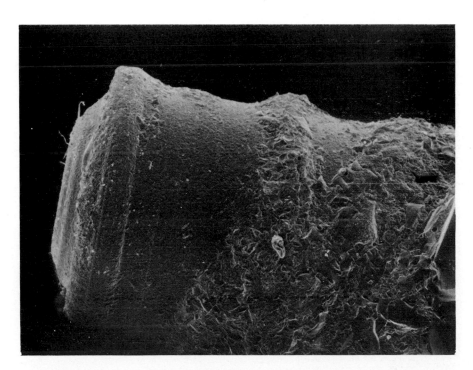

1b. Collar shapes were produced experimentally while drilling on glass using diamond as an abrasive with a copper rod. The collar can be equated with changes in the leading edge of the copper drill in which flaring of the copper increases the diameter of the rod.

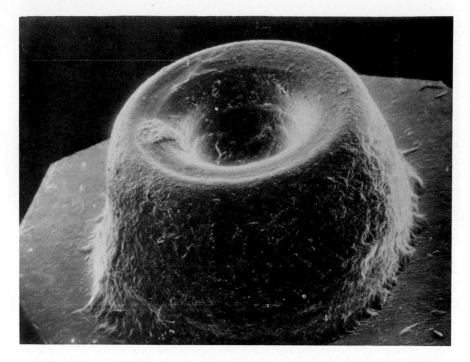

2a. Scanning micrograph of the impression of a tubular copper drill hole in red granite in which wet sand was used as an abrasive. There are no abrasion lines. A similar finding occurred with crushed quartz. No lines were produced when olive oil or a contemporary lubricant were used.

2b. Abrasion lines were evident on the inner and outer walls of the drill hole where emery was used as an abrasive. These occurred when the emery was used wet, with olive oil or a contemporary lubricant. Fine lines can be seen at the leading edge (arrow) which appears smooth and rounded.

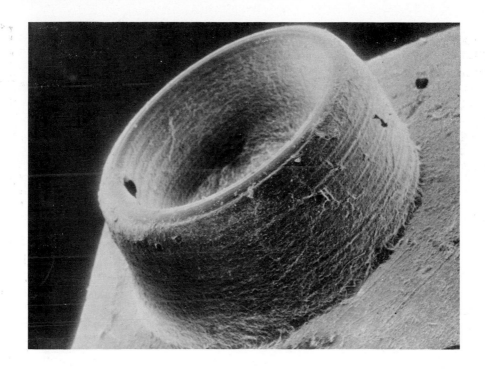

3a & b. Scanning micrographs of impression taken from holes in red granite which were made with a tubular copper drill and corundum (a) and diamond (b). Lines similar to those found when emery was used are evident. It would be of interest to determine the pattern produced by beryl and topaz (Mohs 8).

4. The Mohs scale of hardness modified by Woodall helps to explain the results found in drilling granite. Emery, corundum and diamond whose hardness is 9, 9 and 10 respectively all produced concentric lines when used wet, with olive oil and a contemporary lubricant. Sand and quartz with a Mohs value at 7 and similar to granite did not produce abrasion lines. Note that diamond is four times harder than emery or corundum.

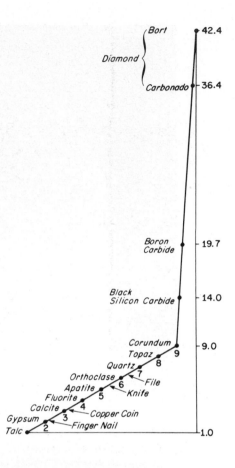

5. Scanning micrograph of a drill hole made in glass using silicon carbide as an abrasive bonded to a copper rod using hide glue and sodium silicate (water glass). The tracking due to fixation of the abrasive particles produces regular, circumferential lines in the glass.

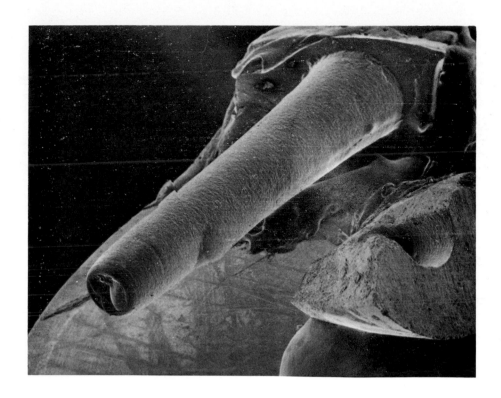

6a & b. Scanning micrographs of an impression of the incomplete drill hole in an agate seal of the Achaemenid period. Evidence for the use of a tubular drill stems from the distinct fracture pattern at the base of the hole due to removal of the core. Note the rounding of the leading edge and its relatively smooth character.

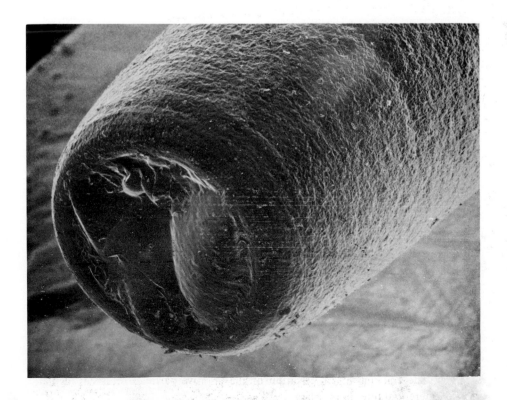

7a & b. Scanning micrographs of an impression of an experimental drill hole made in an agate slab using a tubular copper drill and diamond as an abrasive. Note the appearance of the base due to fracture of the core and its subsequent removal. Also note the similarity of the leading edge of the drilling with that of the agate seal, i.e., rounding and smoothening of the site. Abrasion lines are more frequent suggesting the use of another abrasive for drilling the seal.

1. The Miqnêyaw seal: above, obverse and sealing; below, reverse and sealing.

2. The Miqnêyaw seal: enlargement of the obverse side.

3. The Miqnêyaw seal: enlargement of the reverse.

4. A Drawing of the inscriptions of the seal of Miqnêyaw
(the reverse is drawn as it would appear on a bulla).

1. Seal of Shemaʻ servant of Yarobʻam from Megiddȯ, first half of the 8th century B.C.E. R. Hestrin and M. Dayagi-Mendels, *Inscribed Seals: First Temple Period, Hebrew, Ammonite, Moabite, Phoenician and Aramaic from the Collections of the Israel Museum and the Israel Department of Antiquities and Museums*, Jerusalem, 1979, no. 3, (IDAM, cast no. 230).

2. Seal impression of ʼElyaqim [serv] ant of YWKN on pottery jar handle, Ramat Raḥel. Late 8th century B.C.E. R. Hestrin and M. Dayagi-Mendels, *Inscribed Seals*, no. 9, (IDAM 64-1771).

3. Seal of ʼElyashib son of ʼEshyahu. Arad. Late 7th century B.C.E. R. Hestrin and M. Dayagi-Mendels, *Inscribed Seals*, no. 11, (IDAM 67-663).

4. Pottery jar handle stamped with *lamelekh* and "private" seals. Ramat Raḥel. Late 8th century B.C.E. R. Hestrin and M. Dayagi-Mendels, *Inscribed Seals*, no. 18, (IDAM 63-39).

2 Cylinder seal worn on a necklace. Stele B of Naram-Sin (ca. 2250 B.C.) from Susa, originally from Sippar (detail). Reproduced from P. Amiet, *L'Art Antique du Proche Orient* (1977), p. 134 fig. 49, by permission of the publisher, Editions d'Art Lucien Mazenod (Paris).

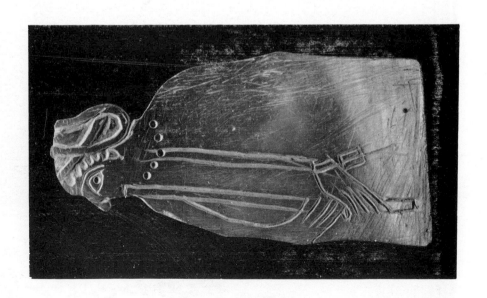

1 Cylinder seal worn on a bracelet (?). Mother-of-pearl inlay from Nippur, EDIIIa (ca. 2800 B.C.). Courtesy of the Metropolitan Museum of Art, Rogers Fund, 1962, 62.70.46. Reference courtesy Elizabeth Williams-Forte.